BEING A WIFE

JUST GOT REAL?

I loved the conversational aspect of *Being a Wife Just Got Real*, which I think will be big for readers who are not usually non-fiction readers. I think you have a hit on your hands.

—Victoria Christopher Murray, Author, 2016 NAACP Image Award for Outstanding Literary Work, Fiction

I love the way *Being a Wife Just Got Real* is written. It is as if I am literally having a real live conversation with Tanya. This was so entertaining. Even though I've been married over ten years and my hubby and I are in a really good place, I was nodding my head because I could already relate to so much of what Tanya said she's been through in the early years of her marriage.

—Christine St. Vil, Author, Speaker, Digital Strategist

What a wonderful book! I see myself in *Being a Wife Just Got Real*, even at the ripe, old age of 78. I enjoyed reading it because it made it clear that most of us do not have a clue of what being a wife is all about. Up until the last three years, I realized that I struggled the first 58 years of my marriage. I now see that with God's help, wives can steer the direction of our marriages from the very beginning.

—Violet Carter

Being a Wife Just Got Real was one of the most refreshing reads I have experienced in a while. The book's clarity and authenticity is what I enjoyed the most. I loved that while I was reading it, I experienced every emotion possible;

I laughed more than anything. I empathized not just with Tanya, but also with Don. The beauty in this story is that if Don never had a "Tanya" and vice versa, they would have never healed from their individual deep-rooted issues that would have otherwise stayed buried. Congratulations on your first book. WELL DONE!

—Pastor Portia Taylor,
Victory Christian Ministries International – Waldorf

Being a Wife Just Got Real is an inside look into the life of a woman living her own "war room" experience. It shines the light on just how marriage quickly becomes work (ministry) after the fairytale of the wedding is over. This book gets more real as it goes along. It's candid enough, that as a reader, you find yourself and your mate within the narrative.

—Sherryle Kiser Jackson, Multi-published Christian author of *Soon and Very Soon* and *The Land of Promiscuity*.

BEING A WIFE
JUST GOT REAL

Things I Wish I Knew Before I Said "I Do"

TANYA BARNETT

Washington, DC 20016

Published by Tanya's Xchange
White Plains, Maryland
TanyasXchange.com

Printed in the United States of America

Front cover photograph – Ladyreddcreationsphotography.org
Back cover photograph – Eyeimagery.zenfolio.com
Book jacket design and branding – www.julianbkiganda.com
Make up – Beautiful Faces, Keshua Hunt

ISBN   978-0997493702 (pbk.)
Library of Congress Control Number   2016907087

Dedication

This book is to honor my maternal grandmother,
Ruth Westcott James. During the summers, my brothers
and I stayed with our grandparents in the country where I
watched my grandmother take care of my granddaddy,
Chester James.

Every day, my grandmother always had three hot meals
waiting for my granddaddy. I vividly remember that in the
evenings, when he came home covered in dust from riding
on a tractor all day, he could count on a fresh meal waiting
for him. She showed her love for him in such a soft and
caring way. I don't remember my grandparents saying
much to each other, but they had an unspoken love
everyone could feel.

I recently found out my grandmother was a firecracker in
her younger days and that it took years for that grace and
elegance as a wife to come out. My prayer is that God will
grace me to live long enough to do the same.

Because you are holding this book, I want you to know you
are one special lady and I also dedicate this book to you. My
hope for you is that this book will encourage you no matter
where you are in your marriage.

Whether you are single, engaged, a newlywed, have 20
years in, or even divorced, this book was written
specifically for you. Whether you laugh out loud because of
the stories or silently reflect on lessons I learned, my prayer
is that you will put your big girl panties on and grow up to
be the good thing that God has called you and me to be:

A wife.

Table of Contents

BEING A WIFE
JUST GOT REAL

Things I Wish I Knew Before I Said "I Do"

TANYA BARNETT

Acknowledgements

Without my Lord and Savior, Jesus Christ, I would not still be married to my husband, Donald. I thank God daily for being the source of my strength. I am thankful that I was smart enough to seek Him in the midst of those days when I just did not think I could do this wife thing another second. He gave me the courage to fight for my marriage and to love my husband, even when I did not want to. I rejoice that I can now say that my husband is truly my lover and my best friend.

The file for this book sat on my desktop for over two years until I met my fabulous mentor, Julian B. Kiganda, of Bold & Fearless. At the time, she was a ray of much-needed light in my life. One day, in the midst of one of our many conversations, she said, "Girl, you have a story to tell; you need to write a book."

Immediately, my eyes lit up! I shared with her that I started writing a book a few years back and that I never got past the second chapter. I told her I stopped working on it because I was not sure if anyone would even read it, let alone buy it.

When I realized Julian was interested in it, I asked her if I could send it to her. Of course, she said,

"Yes." Within a week, she called and said, "Girl, this could be a bestseller! What are you waiting for?" I was shocked by her response since she is an author who moves within the circles of today's movers and shakers. She gave me less than a year to get it done. Talk about pressure! The accountability was crucial, but God knew I needed it. Julian, thank you so much for pushing me to finish what I started.

Thank you Big Poppa, Boo-ski, My Omega-Man, honey! If you did not choose me to be your wife, there would be no book. During the process of writing this book, I reflected, cried, and apologized to you so much that you got sick of me. I am grateful we have grown tremendously during our marriage. I am thankful that you were comfortable enough and trusted me enough to allow me to share our story with the world. I love what we have become—a *team*.

I want to thank my parents, Rodney and Ruth Walker, for supporting me in my many endeavors. I know Don and I surprised you by remaining married longer than one year. We love you for praying for us and for not giving up on us. Look at us now. Thank you!

I want to thank my brothers, Rodney and DeVaun, for always supporting me. Your weekly calls to check on me during the writing process were priceless. I appreciate the two of you.

To Mimi W.: Thank you for being there for so many years. Your nonjudgmental support was, and still is, priceless. Before I make decisions, I periodically hear your voice. We shared so many moments and your prayers carried me through it all. I love you, girly! You know, you're the reason I'm still married.

To Shelly R.: We've known each other since kindergarten. For years, you helped me see the humor in the midst of the ugly marriage stuff. Thank you, girl, for always turning my frowns upside down during our numerous two-to-three-hour conversations about our kids and husbands. You are truly my sister from another mother.

To Dion B.: My personal and mighty prayer warrior. Your out-of-the-blue phone calls would constantly be right on time, every time. You always said my marriage had a purpose and even when things were all over the place, you were steadfast in your prayers. Look at the fruit of your prayers, girl. I love you so much!

To Tony Z.: You gave me the first glimpse of my husband's heart. Through our many heated conversations, I learned so much about men. Thank you for all those times you literally told me to "shut up" when I was making situations worse. I love you so much for being man enough and loving us enough to school me on the realness of being the wife my husband needed. You are my brother for life.

To Nicole G. L.: Thank you for real "couch time" moments. When I made those desperate middle of the night phone calls, you told me to come right over and never charged me one thin dime. I appreciate you for listening to me and then encouraging me to do things differently to get different results.

To Tiffany R.: You are a rare gem that I cherish. You are constantly teaching me something new about how to be a better wife. I know for a fact, your advice is from God. I am daily working to put your advice to action. Thank you, honey bun!

Thank you to my awesome pastors, Demond and Portia Taylor of Victory Christian Ministries International–Waldorf. You two are an amazing example of a godly marriage. I love your honesty and transparency in and out of the pulpit. You not only teach us the word - you live it. Our marriage has been the best it has ever been since we joined VCMI–Waldorf. Don and I are forever grateful!

Preface

A few years ago, I woke up with three words stuck in my brain: "Tell Your Story." At the time, I kind of thought those words came from God but I had no idea why He was saying them to me nor what story He was referring to. I literally told Him to, "Stop playing."

Well, you know how it goes, I continued to hear those words throughout the entire day. Whenever that thought invaded my mind, I quickly pushed it away. After all, I was a busy woman who had a long To-Do list to complete.

When I was finally settled down from my super-hectic day, the thought popped in my mind again. At that point, I knew I would get no peace. Even though I tried my hardest to ignore it, I threw my hands up, broke down, and surrendered to the Voice that evening.

With much attitude and a hint of annoyance in my heart, I asked God what exactly was this story I was supposed to be telling. Suddenly, a burning bush and a mighty rush of wind appeared. (That's not really what happened, but I like the way that sounded).

Actually, He gently whispered, "Do you remember those times you prayed to me in the darkest moments of your marriage?" I anxiously replied, "Yes."

In my mind, I was thinking, "What does that have to do with the price of tea in China? It was so long ago." His simple response was, "I want you to share those experiences with other women."

I will not allow you time to even guess how I responded because you know, I immediately went into panic mode. All sorts of thoughts ran through my mind. My first thought was that there was no way I could share those dark moments in a book. What if my dad read the book? He would seriously do bodily harm to Don the next time he saw him.

What if people began to think the worst of my husband? Or worse, what if they thought that I was a stupid fool for staying with this man? A few of our friends knew we had issues in those early years, but they never knew to what extent. Sharing those painful moments would reveal to the world that we used to be a hot mess.

I rationalized that there was no way I had heard from God. Besides, if I shared my story, my husband would be embarrassed and would never be able to show his face around town again. I just knew there was no way he would consent to me telling the ugly truth about what went on behind our closed doors.

We all know that you do not air your dirty laundry, especially if you are a Christian. I immediately assumed he would not understand that I was instructed by God to put our early years of marriage in a book. After having several conversations with myself, I pushed the idea of writing this book out of my mind.

A few months later, that nagging feeling came back. After the kids went to bed and Don was downstairs in his man cave, I closed my bedroom door and entered "The Zen Zone" (my place of quiet solitude). In there, I mustered enough courage to power on my tablet. I was nervous, but I totally surrendered to God's voice.

As I began to type those first few words, I had no idea what I was going to talk about. Surprisingly, the first chapter was typed within an hour. When I reread the words on the screen, I could not believe they came from me. They sounded like they were written by a "real" author. I continued to let the words flow out of me onto the screen, so by the next day, chapter two was just being formed.

I saved the file and made plans to revisit it later that week. Well, that didn't happen. Without warning, the book came to a screeching halt. Before I knew it, I was caught up in living a hectic life and quite frankly, I forgot about the file that contained this book.

Two years went by before I looked at the file again. I had a deep down, gut feeling that I needed to get this book written, immediately. Thanks to Julian's encouragement, I gained the courage to open the file. I realized that my experiences were not any different than other wives, so I knew sharing them would show women that they were not alone.

A few weeks later, I spoke with Julian about going forward with completing the book. She suggested I speak to Don first, to see if he was okay with me writing a book about our marriage. I prayed for about a week before I approached him. You know I had to prepare the perfect atmosphere before talking to him about exposing our "crazy" behavior for all the world to see.

At first, he had a million and one questions, which irritated me. However, I patiently sat there and answered every one of them. After I read the first chapter to him, he freaked out. He said that I made him look like a monster. I sweetly told him, "You were but that's not who you are now." I could tell he wasn't comfortable with what I wrote but I silently prayed that he would acquiesce. He asked me to give him a few days to think about it; which I did.

About a week later, Don came to me with his blessing with the condition that he read it along the way. I was super excited that he was on-board with the book coming to life. I sent Julian a text to say I was going forward with the book, in which, she gave me a January 2016 due date. I finished the rough draft in July 2015.

My initial thoughts never made it into this book because the writing process took on a life of its own. Instead of glossing over our issues, I was challenged with being totally transparent. In my being transparent and honest, I knew it would be a blessing to you. Please understand that every word you read was written with you in mind.

I want you to laugh out loud at our wild and crazy antics when we were clueless, young newlyweds. My desire is that this book will encourage you to want to become a better version of you which will lead to you becoming a better wife, whether you are currently one or not.

Ultimately, my hope is to leave you with powerful nuggets and realistic tips to ponder and to use for years to come. This book is all about you and how

God's grace and mercy can empower you to implement positive change in your life today!

Please take your time when going through this book. I intentionally made sure the size was large enough to write in and small enough to fit in your purse. I placed reflection questions, prayers and a section to write down your thoughts or personal prayer requests at the end of each chapter.

I really want you to use these tools. Write dates next to your prayer requests and then go back and write the date those prayers were answered. If things pop out at you while reading, write all up in this book and then let me know via social media; my contact information is in Chapter Seven. I urge you to be proactive in being the agent of change for not only yourself, but for your family and your community.

Now, grab a pen, some tissues and your favorite snack (mine is Flaming Hot Cheetos dipped in partially frozen chocolate pudding). Find a quiet, comfy place to join me on a journey back to my first years of being a wife - because, girlfriend, this thing just got real!

1 What The Heck Is A Wife Anyway?

The man who finds a wife, finds a treasure, and he receives favor from the LORD. —Proverbs 18:22 (NLT)

That seems like a really stupid question, right? After all, the world has been filled with wives since the first wife, Eve. My Momma and my Daddy have been married for more than 45 years. My grandmothers and most of my aunts were wives until "death did they part." My other aunts are still married to their husbands. One would be led to believe that because I grew up with such awesome examples, I, of all people, would know what the definition of a wife was.

Well, I really didn't know exactly what one was nor did I realize the extent of the duties and responsibilities (yes, you read correctly, responsibilities) entailed to be a good wife. All I knew was that I was picking out cute wedding invitations, going shopping for a really fabulous wedding dress and that I was marrying a super cute guy, with freckles, who adored me. Yup! That was it! What more did I need? Honey, clearly, I had no idea.

Webster's Dictionary defines a wife as "a married woman," "a female partner in a marriage." Wow! Webster! Really? That's all we get? It seems very strange to me that there are no other definitions for the word "wife."

Could it possibly be that Noah Webster knew that if he did not accurately come up with a definition for the word "wife," he would have to hear his wife Rebecca's mouth? After all, they did have eight children that she was home with while he travelled the United States.

I can imagine how that conversation went. While bouncing her newborn on her hip, she probably looked at him very innocently and with the sweetest voice she asked, "Noah, dear, what is your definition of the word wife?"

I will assume he felt a humungous amount of pressure at that very moment and in a rush to stay in her good graces and to get out of the hot seat, he most likely blurted out the most benign response ever, "Um, well, of course, a married woman, honey!" I can just see her roll her eyes as she huffed off to tend to the kids arguing over who was going to ride the hobby horse next. Smart man!

What I've learned in the 17 years that I have been married is that in reality, wives are extremely: flexible, patient, giving, loving, forgiving, strong, and practical in various situations and circumstances. This is not a conclusive list, heck, it barely scratches the surface of what wives are, but it is a great starting point.

If you are single, you are probably just as eager to get married and equally as clueless as I was. If you are married, I am sure you can come up with some of your own definitions for the roles you play as a wife. If you are divorced or widowed, I am certain you can share with me the roles you played and, most definitely, could teach me a thing or two.

In 1999, I clearly had a fairy tale idea of what my marriage was going to look like. I believe I was under the impression that I would be a glorified girlfriend with the perks of having this man share my home during the day and my warm bed at night. We would passionately love each other day in and day out, always work together as a team, and be totally harmonious until "death did we part."

Soon after saying, "I do," I quickly discovered that my fantasy idea was far from reality. I realized there would be days when my husband and I would be arch enemies and there would be days we would be battle buddies.

During the early years, my husband and I were the urban version of, The War of The Roses. When I watched this movie, I was overcome with sadness. It was eye opening and revealed how two people, who once professed their never-ending love to each other, slowly became so self-centered in a marriage, their love evolved into distain for each other. That was who Don and I had become.

We were also living in a perpetual state of the movie, The Story of Us, which was so profound to me. Michelle Pfeiffer and Bruce Willis perfectly portrayed our marriage on the big screen. I have never watched the movie in the allotted time. Every time I attempted to watch it, I always paused to reflect, cried and then hit rewind. It was a true depiction of us and our foolishness. We would love each other in the morning and then hate each other by lunch time.

Praise God! I can now say that I am my husband's helper, partner, teacher, friend, nurse, coach, intercessor, etc. All in all, wives should be our husbands' Best Friend Forever (BFF), you know, until we are 100-years-old-type of forever.

I know some of you are thinking, "Tanya, you don't know my husband. What you're saying sounds cool for you, but it's not even remotely possible for us." That's okay; I get it. If someone said these things to me three weeks into my new marriage, they would have gotten the same response from me.

What I found is that God has blessed wives with the privilege and honor to see their husbands in their most vulnerable moments. Yes, I said privilege and honor. Seeing them this way is intimate and private and should never be shared. I was not prepared for that. I never saw my dad sad, scared, nor sick. If he was ever beat up by life's circumstances, I never knew it. I assumed all men were "strong" like my daddy. Boy, was I in for a rude awakening.

Over time, I learned that it is at these times that we must allow them to shed off the male bravado and allow them to be vulnerable with us. I remember plenty times when Don would call me from his car during his workday because he was stressed out. He felt like he could not get through some days without losing his cool or quitting his job. I would oftentimes be quiet and just listen to him vent. Other times, I would give him advice on how to get through the rest of his day.

It is in these moments that we are supposed to help build him up, even when we do not want to. Besides, if we do not allow our husbands to be vulnerable with us, trust and believe, the ultra-sexy floozy at work or the lonely cheer mom with a fresh batch of homemade cupcakes is just waiting to be his confidant and more. I can say this because I was the lonely cheer mom but more about that later.

I also discovered that we have to step back and allow our husbands the space to be stupid and irrational (for lack of better words). Note to self: when we get to popping off at the mouth and arguing back, we make matters worse. Raise your hand if you are that chick who had a hand in creating this phenomenon. Well, you will soon learn tips to not only avoid this but to also alleviate these types of situations.

For years, I was an incessant Chihuahua. I would literally chase Don from room to room to make sure I got the last word in an argument and then be shocked when he fired off a string of obscenities to get me to leave him alone. I would then have the audacity to stand there, with an indignant look on my face and my arms crossed because I couldn't believe that he just went off on me. Really? This was so childish and immature. I am still embarrassed by the fact that I did this for so many years.

After these heated moments pass (let's own that some we contributed to), our husbands will need time and space to come to their senses and to apologize for their actions or inactions. After they get their minds right, we need to forgive them even if they do not apologize; even if we feel they do not deserve our forgiveness. Forgiveness is for us anyway.

When our husbands have extremely bad days, we should be there to support them and to reassure them that we have their backs. When we do this selfless act, we teach them they can trust us with their most intimate feelings without judgment. We have to be their friend and give them our shoulders to cry on.

The greatest benefit of being a wife is the ability to nurse them back to wholeness while easing their minds with our sexual healing. This is a fact. Get over it, girlfriend! Men need sex. Women need sex.

We are here to help our husbands release stress and to reconnect with them. The reality is that if our husbands cannot release with us, their needs do not simply disappear because we have a headache, an attitude or the kids have mountains of homework.

Maybe if you had sex with your husband instead of being frustrated, the headache and attitude would go away. He may even offer to help the kids with their homework afterwards (it works for me every time). I'm just keeping it real.

Sexual intimacy with our husbands is a gift God has given us. If we wise up and stop seeing it as a chore, we would see how much we can look forward to it. This takes a perspective change. I look at it like this, I have to do it anyway, so I might as well gain the benefits from it! Hey, it's a gift that keeps on giving, so enjoy it! Try something different—they like that. Put those kids to bed early, dust off your Jodeci or Maxwell CDs and then take a bath together, tonight.

We must also use our encouraging words to coach them back to feeling empowered enough to face the world after disappointments. Our love for them should give us the desire to pray for them. If you are not there yet, no judgments against you. It took years for me to pray for my husband solely because of my unconditional love for him, not out of frustration with him.

There will be times when you want to spend every waking moment cuddling and making love to your honey, and there will also be times when you will want to spend every waking moment away from him on a cruise ship to the Grecian Island with your girlfriends. I totally get it. I feel that way too sometimes.

Wives have been given the privilege to see beyond the male bravado front they put up for the world and their friends. We have the ability to see them the way God sees them, if we choose to. This is key! We have a choice to make. We have to make an intentional decision to see them through God's eyes; after all, they are God's children and gifts to us.

I do not want to preach to you because I know I will lose you if I do that. However, I have to be honest with you: being a loving and compassionate wife is a choice and is something that should not be taken lightly.

It takes work. It takes dedication. It takes time. It takes love. This book is filled with nuggets to help you embrace the beauty in your marriage. I want you to fight for (not with) your husband and your marriage.

Guess who said "Yes" when he proposed? You. Guess who ran around showing all their girlfriends that he finally put a ring on it? You. And, guess who posted selfies all over social media of that ring? You. Guess who planned that elaborate wedding? Let's be honest, You. Finally, guess who convinced him to go to the Justice of

Peace before he had time to change his mind? That's right, sister, You.

You fell in love with his quirky ways. You believed he was your Prince Charming found in Harlequin Romance and Zane books. You loved his comprehensive package. You fell in love with "Mr. Right" who just happened to also be an imperfect guy.

Even Prince Charming can't be perfect all the time. He will have ways that irritate you beyond your wildest irritation. He will not value everything you place value on. His family could possibly work your last nerve. He may even leave his dirty socks on the bedroom floor and burp without saying, "Excuse me."

Newsflash: You're not perfect either. Yes, missy ma'am, I said that! You are not perfect and neither am I. You and I both have quirky ways that our guys thought were cute when we were dating them. All that cuteness now seems to get on their nerves too.

I could care less about how many designer purses you own or what car you drive. I do not care what your title is at work. You could very well be the devil who wears Prada and not even know it.

I know you are probably rolling your eyes at me, but it's cool. Trust me, you will get over it by the time you finish reading this book! Because you know what? I was the devil who wore flip flops, baggy shirts, mom jeans and stayed home with two kids under two years old.

Instead of focusing on your shortcomings, I'd rather focus on how strong you are. First of all, you are one courageous woman. Marriage is a major commitment that you don't throw away because it's not picture perfect. None of them are and if anyone tells you theirs is, they are lying.

I truly believe that anyone who wants to be married must be informed with the truth about what really happens, prepared for the ups and downs and up for the challenge of trusting God to see you through the good and the bad. Those who remain married beyond the first twenty-four hours of saying, "I do," have got to be strong women.

I am aware that some of us tried to keep our marriages together, however, they eventually ended in divorce for whatever reason. Sis, you are not a failure. My pastor once said that if something does not work out, view that experience as data collection. Learn from it instead of letting it define you. I would even challenge you to look internally to see what you can do today to prepare yourself for your future husband, if that is your desire. I truly believe marriage is a tool that reveals to us who we really are.

I also need you to understand that marriage is a full-time job. It is extremely hard work, but it is a worthy investment towards a fulfilling and lifelong partnership. If a husband and wife are intentional about putting the time and energy into their marriage, everyone benefits, including your awesome children.

So, by now, I know you're thinking, "Whew, Tanya, I need a nap. I don't know if I am ready for this marriage thing after reading this chapter. I may just join a convent and audition for Sister Act." I would say to you, be open-minded to receive the messages in this book. Not only will you be a great wife, you can and will have a great marriage.

If you're married, you are most likely thinking, "Tanya, this can't be all there is to my marriage. I want my loving Prince Charming back. I just don't see how things can improve." With my hand on my hip, I'm saying to you, "Honey, if I can do it, you can do it. You have never been married to Donald Barnett, so give me just a few minutes of your time."

Reflection

• Why the heck do I want to get married? Why the heck did I marry my husband?

_____

_____

_____

• Write down the five things you love the most about your man. Take a few moments to reflect on your love for him. If you are not married, what are some characteristics you are looking for?

_____

_____

_____

_____

• List things you anticipate going into marriage. List things you did not anticipate. Compare the two lists. Are they realistic? If not, why?

_____

_____

_____

Prayer

Thank you, Lord, for the gift of marriage. Your Word says that marriage is a mystery. I surrender and admit that I am clueless about being a wife. Thank you for your divine wisdom to become the best me and a better wife! I declare that my (future) marriage is an example of love, patience, and kindness for my family and friends.

Remove any unrealistic expectations I had. I now realize they are set ups for disappointments. Help me love my fiancé/husband just the way he is, without trying to change him. Because you love me with all my imperfections, I choose to love him and all his imperfections too.

I trust you to develop my fiancé/husband into the man of God that I need. Help us to always choose loving words and actions with each other. Teach us to daily build each other up as we live this marriage journey.

Bless the children that you gift our family with, whether they are biological or not. Thank you for their lives. Give us wisdom to raise them to be honest and kind. They will know you as their Savior and Lord. We will be godly examples of a husband and wife for the people we interact with daily.

In Jesus' name, Amen!

Thoughts/Prayer Requests

_____

_____

_____

_____

_____

_____

_____

_____

_____

_____

_____

_____

_____

_____

_____

_____

_____

_____

_____

_____

_____

_____

2 Two Words: Donald Barnett

"Marriage is not a noun; it's a verb. It isn't something you get. It's something you do. It's the way you love your partner every day." —Barbara De Angelis

I know my girlfriends and my mom are laughing hysterically at the title of this chapter. For whatever reason, they refer to my husband as Donald Barnett. I think because he is such a character and his presence is so big, that it only seems proper to call him by his government name. For months, I wrestled with the title of this chapter, but I knew that it had to be Donald Barnett. By the time you finish this book, you will most likely agree.

In March 1998, I met Don at my job. People would call it a coincidence: he had a doctor's appointment on the first day of work of my new job. I call it a God set-up because I was not supposed to even start this job until the following week. The doctor called me Thursday night to ask me if I could come in to receive training Friday morning instead of the following Monday. It was also my husband's first appointment at this doctor's office.

Side note: To set the record straight and to make my husband happy, I am putting into print for all the world to see that I, Tanya Barnett, do solemnly swear that, yes, I did give him my cell phone, my apartment, and my parents' home number before he left the doctor's office that day. There Donald Barnett! You happy?

Now back to the story: Initially, I liked Don. I loved his freckles and the fact that he loved to take me out to eat. He also got extra brownie points because he took my daughter and me out to dinner almost every weekend. Don had a natural sense of humor that kept me laughing all the time and my parents and my daughter loved him.

However, after a few months, my infatuation wore off. I actually began to become irritated with him. In my eyes, he became annoying. He came to my job almost daily to bring me either a cheap $.99 rose from 7-11 (you know the one that has the plastic water cap on the bottom of it), a salad or some other thing like Reese's Cups. Can you believe I allowed this to irritate me instead of realizing that he really liked me?

Don eventually gave up pursuing me after I stopped returning his calls. I was no longer interested in him and besides, he ran up my cell phone bill by calling me all the time! At that time, there were no data plans or packages. Each call a person made was paid by the minute. For months, I harassed him for that $200.

Come to think of it, I don't think I ever got that money back from him. Hold that thought while I text him to PayPal me that $200.

Okay, I'm back; the transfer is complete. It only took 17 years to get that money back.

By May, I ran Don off with my "Miss Independent" and "I don't need you" attitude. Once we officially broke up, I decided I would remain a single mom and not get married. I truly believed I would never get married and I was okay with it. I felt like I did not need a relationship to tie me down and because they seemed like a lot of work; which in reality, they are.

I had been a single mom for six years with no help from anyone besides my parents. All my bills were paid, my six-year-old daughter, Gabrielle, was in private school, and I had a three-bedroom apartment with a roommate. Gab's father was in and out of jail, so he was not in her life. I was fine with that because she still had my dad.

In my eyes, my single life was great. I decided I would go out on the weekends and enjoy my freedom without the headache of someone wondering what I was doing or if he could come to see me. I would not have the headache of commitment nor have the headache of security. I would not have the headache of someone having my back 24/7. (Note: there is plenty of sarcasm and eye rolling in the last two sentences).

I went on my merry way, not even giving Donald Barnett another thought; my grandma would have said, "I ain't even studying him." Soon after that, I started seeing another guy. I deceived myself into thinking I was using this guy for going out on my terms or whenever I had time but in reality, he was using me. I was in denial of just how dysfunctional this relationship was and how I was not valuing myself at all.

I was with him just for the sake of having a man who treated me right. He was a college graduate, had a good paying job, a car, and took me to expensive restaurants to eat. He clearly was not ringing my phone all the time like Donald Barnett did. I was doing this thing on my terms, girlfriend, or so I thought.

Looking back after all these years, I realize this guy never valued me. He never introduced me to one person he knew. He never asked to meet my daughter. He never took me out to eat anywhere close to where we lived and he never saw me during the day. He would come to my apartment after my daughter fell asleep and left before the sun came up.

After four months of that, I asked about becoming his girlfriend, but he said he was not ready for one. I allowed this to continue for a few more weeks but in the midst of it, I became frustrated and angry. It felt like my plan was backfiring on me. I kept telling myself I was going to make him bring me around his friends the next time we got together. This never happened.

He, on the other hand, was cool with the way things were. He said he liked that I was fun to be with and did not stress him out like other women had done. He claimed that he wished more women were mature like me and knew how to let a man have his space. This dude even had the nerve to play Kenny Lattimore's, "With You," the next time I saw him.

He told me I was special in his eyes and that I was "wife" material. You know my ears perked up when I heard that magical four-letter word. In my mind, those were the code words for "We are about to become an item."

At the time, I did not realize that he only told me things I wanted to hear to shut me down from saying the G-word: girlfriend. I tried to convince myself that I was okay with our situation but each day this dragged on, I became resentful and began to hate what I was doing.

One Sunday morning, I woke up and said to myself, "I can't be in this relationship anymore." I knew there had to be more for my life than working 12-hour night shifts, going to school, doing homework with Gab, and sporadically seeing this guy. At that point, I realized that I did want more. I wanted a real relationship. I wanted someone to love me and my child.

I decided to go to church because I was feeling down about telling my friend he could not come over the night before. I got Gabi dressed and said a little prayer as I drove to church. Needless to say, I cried the entire service.

Wouldn't you know that the message was tailor made just for me? The pastor spoke about Jesus being your source of peace and joy, not external things such as material things, people or whatever else we gravitate towards to gain immediate comfort.

I sat there thinking, "Who told the pastor my business? How did he know I was miserable and felt empty inside?" When they opened the altar up for prayer, I took that long walk up to the front of the church. I cried so badly, that one of the ushers had to walk me to another room until I got myself together. Thank goodness Gabi was in children's church.

On my way home, I replayed past relationships with men over and again in my mind. Not one of them had been healthy. There was never any mutual respect. I was always the one giving my time, money and energy to keep those relationships going. I was the one calling them, not the other way around; except, Donald Barnett.

When I got home from church, I made the decision that I would not allow these types of relationships to dictate my happiness ever again. I was tired of pretending that I had great relationships.

After all, my friends thought I was lucky to be with this guy since he was cute and drove a Lexus—what more did you need? I decided that I was totally done with these dead end relationships and that I would never again be someone's booty call.

I called him and told him that I could not continue with this relationship. His reply was, "Are you sure? If you are, I'm cool with it." He was not even phased by what I said. He simply kept it moving. Isn't that some bull? In hindsight, it was actually a blessing and a major turning point in my single life.

By November 1998, Mr. "You Know Who" reappeared in my life: Donald Barnett. He called my job to speak to the doctor, who was with another patient. I had to talk to him since I was the only medical technician in the office and the protocol was that I handled patient inquiries when the doctor was unavailable.

After I scheduled Don an appointment with the doctor, we chitchatted for a few awkward moments. He asked if he could call me on my cell phone and after I said "Yes," we decided we would continue the conversation that evening.

Don called me later that night and I immediately knew this man was my future husband. I honestly cannot tell you how I knew this. I just felt a tug deep down in my belly. Since I had this great revelation, I couldn't wait to share it with him before the phone call ended.

I excitedly blurted out, "God said you are going to be my husband!" This joker had the nerve to say, "Really? The Lord didn't tell me anything, so I will wait to hear from Him." I was so embarrassed, that I didn't bring it up again but I knew in my spirit this was my husband. Don proposed to me soon after.

In January 2000, we set a June 2000 wedding date. Soon after that, Don took Gabi and me to Pennsylvania to meet his Grannie and the rest of the family. They instantly received Gabi and I into the family. Before I knew it, we were visiting his family all the time and we loved being with them.

I also met some of his fraternity brothers and was adopted as their sister. A few weeks later, I met his sister and she adopted us too. I was so excited that I was actually getting married and that he had such a great family. I could not wait for June to hurry up and get there.

Don and I only had two months of marriage counseling. That's it. We completed the activities in a workbook, so we just knew we were equipped and ready to be husband and wife. After our eight-week sessions concluded, we knew we wanted four children, where we would live, and how much money we wanted to make. What more did we need to know? (by the way, none of those things we wrote down happened).

We thought those workbook assignments made us ready and prepared to be married. The book was great, but it only touched on surface stuff like, who would take out the trash; not real issues that we would bring into our marriage from our childhood. We did not have a single clue about the realness of marriage.

Six months later, these two totally "polar-opposite ends of the spectrum people" were husband and wife. All I knew about him was that he was raised by his grandmother and his father and that his parents divorced when he was little. That was it. I had no clue about his mom not being in his life. He never shared this with me and it never even dawned on me to ask him about his mother. I know that you're thinking, "This chick is crazy." I believe I was half crazy and blinded by love.

You know that saying, "A man will treat you like he treats his momma?" Well, Donald Barnett had no relationship with his mother, so he truly had no clue or examples of how to treat a wife. Most of his adult relatives had either never been married or had been divorced. His great grandparents were married 70+ years before his great-grandmother passed away. He has a vague memory of their relationship.

Looking back on it, I think if I had known this prior to getting married, I would have suggested that he attend some type of counseling for his mom not being in his life. The hurt he hid from me all those years was literally driving him mad.

I had no idea he was struggling with rejection and abandonment issues because of his mother not being in his life. During the early years of our marriage, I caught the brunt of all that hurt, rejection, and anger. I'll share more about that and our transformation later in the book.

I, on the other hand, grew up with both my parents, two younger brothers, a dog, and a fenced-in yard in the suburbs. No one in my family had ever been divorced nor had any of my friends' parents. I actually did not hear the word "divorce" until I was in high school. Yeah, I know, I was sheltered.

Yes, my parents argued, but I never saw or heard them disrespect each other. All my friends' parents were married and I never saw them argue either. I truly had no clue what I was in for.

I never saw any men cry either. I think I remember when I was around six or seven-years-old, seeing my daddy cry at his mother's funeral. I had no idea that men had emotional needs though. I had no idea they had moments of doubt. I had no idea they were not always strong.

Don and I had no idea that marriage was a living, breathing entity nor did we realize it required committed work and constant compromise for the greater good of our union. We were ignorant to the fact that there would be really good days and that there would be terribly bad days. The "for sickness and health" part did not apply to us because we were young, right? Wrong.

We were in our honeymoon stage all of three weeks before I uttered the words, "This wife thing just got real." One night, I woke up in excruciating pain. I was crying so hard, I could barely speak. That was the first time I saw Donald Barnett panic. That was the first time I saw him cry. As he cried, he begged me to be okay. I was freaking out just watching him freak out.

Here we were, two grown people, crying like lost kids in the middle of the night. Because of my medical background, I put my medical wits to work, dug deep and told him to relax, even though I was in unbearable pain. At that time, I had no idea how to help him or how to reassure him that I was going to be okay. As a wife, I was thinking, "This dude should be comforting me" but that just was not the case.

This was also my first glimpse of my husband in a vulnerable state. I instructed him to call an ambulance and to find someone to watch Gabi so we could go to the hospital. In that moment, Don had become a completely different person. He stood there like a deer in headlights with tears streaming down his face. I had no idea he was afraid of hospitals.

Days later, he finally confided in me how his grandmother and his dad both went into hospitals and passed away there, but he still did not share that he was terrified of hospitals. We never discussed this during the dating stage nor during any of our marriage counseling sessions. In those few minutes of trying to get to the hospital, he was once again that helpless kid, but this time, he was afraid that this would be my fate too.

By the time we got to the hospital, I was pissed off at Don because he was not giving me the attention I needed. Because I was irritated by all of the doctors coming in and out of my room to examine me, I started ordering Don to get out of their way or to do this or that for me.

My husband could not handle my nasty attitude nor all the doctors' examinations, so he said he was going to leave me there by myself. It was awful. Neither of us had any idea of what to do and there were no textbooks for us to reference for a situation like this one.

After a full day of testing, the medical staff finally diagnosed my pain as a ruptured ovarian cyst. This was only after they took my appendix out by mistake (I know, this was an epic fail). After the surgery, they took me to my room to recover, so I told Don to go home to rest and to check on Gabi since she was with a neighbor.

I was discharged with orders to rest for six weeks. My husband called his cousins in Pennsylvania to see if Gabi could stay with them while I recovered. They eagerly took her since this would give her a few weeks to get to know her new family.

I was looking forward to having time to spend together: just the two of us. We never had an opportunity to do this because we did not go on a honeymoon. We got married on Saturday and went to work on Monday. I knew we needed this time to bond and grow closer to each other.

As old "Murphy's Law" would have it, the bonding never happened. About two weeks later, an ex-boyfriend called our home to congratulate me on my new marriage. Well, guess who answered the phone and ripped him a new one? You guessed it—Donald Barnett. He accused me of all sorts of things, but none of it was true. When he asked if I ever sleep with the guy, I immediately lied and said "No." I wanted to admit that I did, but his reaction to the phone call scared me so much that I blurted out "No" to keep the peace.

Needless to say, my husband began to look for evidence to prove me a liar. He eventually found an old diary of mine that was packed away in the basement in my college trunk. One single entry implicated me. I wrote how I regretted it and how it ruined our friendship. My husband only focused on the sex part, not my regret.

After five weeks of marriage, my husband decided I was not to be trusted. I was devastated. I had no idea what to do or say. I was mentally paralyzed. In one moment, I went from being his beautiful, blushing new wife to a lying, no-good "so and so." He saw me as his enemy and it took years to gain back his trust.

I was not equipped to handle such rejection and anger. I had never experienced anything like this in my entire life. I immediately retreated within myself while he found solace in his frat brothers. I did not tell my friends what was going on; they were still excited about the fact that I got married to this amazing guy. I was at my wit's end and was suffering alone in silence.

This began years of estrangement, anger, resentment, distrust, bitterness, and frustration for the both of us. If I had read a book like this one before I got married, I could have been prepared and equipped with information to weather our storms. It would have saved us so much heartache and years of pain.

My prayer is that this book will help you avoid some of the pitfalls that ruin marriages. Only because of God, did we stick together through so many trials.

Reflection

• I want you to take a few moments to reflect on your life. Put the book down to give yourself time to really think about your past.

• Having reflected on your life, what are some issues that you realize you may be bringing into your marriage or have brought into your marriage? Be honest with yourself and write them down. Pray for God to give you direction as to how to get help to overcome these issues.

_____

_____

_____

• Now, put a big X through those things and declare they no longer have control over your life.

• What was the first major conflict in your marriage? Write it down. How did you resolve it?

_____

_____

_____

• If you did not resolve it, what could you do today to work towards a resolution?

_____

_____

_____

• If you are not married, jot down how you plan to resolve conflict with your future husband.

_____

_____

_____

• Why do you think it is important to have a plan for conflict resolution?

_____

_____

_____

Prayer

Lord, reveal to me any unresolved issues that I may be bringing or those I have brought into my marriage. Help me acknowledge them and then leave them at your feet. I declare, that today, they no longer define me because I am your child and you have set me free.

Your Word says, "I am a new creature in you." Old things in my life have passed away because you have made all things new. Create in me a giving and loving heart.

Thank you for the new life I have in you. Thank you for your fresh anointing that breaks yokes and sets the captives free. I praise you for a new freedom in you. Forgive me for taking my misplaced anger and frustration out on _____. He is not my enemy and I love him dearly.

Prepare _____ and me for a better marriage by allowing us to acknowledge our issues. Teach us to leave them at your feet.

Restore my marriage to what your Word says it is. Give me the heart and mind of Christ. Help me to be more loving and giving to my fiancé/husband.

I know I can do all things through Christ Jesus who strengthens me, so strengthen me to be the wife he needs. I want to love my husband as you have called me to love him. Thank you for the gift of my marriage and the grace to be _____'s wife.

In Jesus' name, Amen!

Thoughts/Prayer Requests

3 Prayer: Couch Time With Jesus

God can do anything, you know—far more than you could ever imagine or guess or request in your wildest dreams! He does it not by pushing us around but by working within us, his Spirit deeply and gently within us. —Ephesians 3:20 (MSG)

One of the main reasons I wrote this book was to share with you the avoidable pain my husband and I inflicted upon each other. I can honestly say that some of the things we said and did were intentional, however, most were not.

Just in case you are single and you did not know this, being a wife gets real after the ceremony ends, the honeymoon is over, half the gifts have been returned for gift cards, and all your friends and family go back to living their lives. My goal is to encourage you as you prepare your heart and mind for a loved-filled and successful marriage. I want you to be a prepared and well-equipped wife who has practical tools to make her marriage work.

If you are already married, I want to encourage you to hang in there and to let you know there will be better days if you earnestly pray focused prayers. I want you to focus on improving yourself first and then allow God to work on your marriage through you. I cannot guarantee that you will see immediate improvements, but I do know that as you mature, your marriage will change. After all, you and your husband are "one," so he benefits from your growth and maturity.

I am also sharing with you what I had to do to stay married. In order for me to endure those tough times, I had to learn how to pray for my husband and my marriage. It was not easy in the beginning and most of the time, I cussed instead of prayed.

To be honest, in the early years of our marriage, cussing won out more times than praying did. I eventually learned to ask God to help me look beyond myself in this marriage thing and to stop cussing Don out. Thankfully, I haven't done that in a long time.

I could not understand why my husband was angry all the time and why I was the recipient of that anger. He was the man that I pledged my love to and who I adored. He was so excited when he asked me to marry him that he started calling me his baby-doll. Now, in his eyes, I was the Bride of Chucky. My mind could not process how he could cuss me out and give me the silent treatment but then ask me to be intimate with him later that night.

I was in a constant state of bewilderment. I was giving this man all my heart and I got nothing but anger in return. Years later, God opened my eyes to see that my marriage was "ministry." He showed me that Donald Barnett needed me to intercede for him and to be a light in his world.

I am so glad I did not give in to the temptation to leave my husband when I felt I could not take one more argument. Who we are now, is not who we were way back then. I praise God that He gave me the desire to want to be a better Tanya and that He gave me the wisdom to seek Him first.

I am going to assume that the reason why you made it to this chapter is because you want to be prepared to be a great wife for your future husband. I also believe my married ladies want to see their marriages not only change, but to see it flourish too. I am proud of them for that. It took me years to get to this point. Prior to that, I was in my own world, causing not only myself heartache and pain, but my husband too.

With that being said, I am going to be honest: I wanted a divorce not even two months into my marriage. I never verbalized it but trust me, sister, I was thinking it 24/7! I felt trapped in a downward spiral. My loving husband was now Dr. Jekyll and Mr. Hyde at the same time, all the time.

My Prince Charming had been oddly replaced by a light-skinned, freckled version of The Hulk. I got so desperate, that I actually went online to see if I was still in the right timeframe to file for an annulment. That was when I stumbled upon a Christian wives' chat room.

I had never even heard of a chat room before that day (that is how you know God was in my marriage from the beginning). In that chat room, I met this awesome lady by the name of Mimi, who would become my best friend. She read my pleas asking for help to get out of this battle zone. Each time I logged into the chat room, she showed up to give me encouraging words. She reassured me things would get better. I honestly had a hard time believing her since she was younger than me.

I also could not see how she could help me get out of this marriage. She suggested we pray together. I never prayed with anybody one on one. I had experienced praying in a group, but I never had a prayer partner. I told her that I would give her a try.

I believed I would do the prayer partner thing so I could have someone to complain to and who would agree with me. I decided to hang on long enough to figure out how to file for an annulment. I did not want to miss the window because I knew a divorce would cost me a boat load of money—something I clearly did not have.

It goes without saying that the first time I prayed with Mimi, I only listened to her. I did not respond with anything other than "Amen." It was awkward, but I remember putting my phone on mute so she could not hear me crying.

I wanted out of my marriage, but she prayed for God to rekindle a love for my husband. She prayed for God to strengthen me. I did not want strength to stay, I wanted strength to leave. She prayed for God to give me direction as to how to be Donald Barnett's wife. I wanted directions and information for my next step to get an annulment.

She prayed that I would honor God in all my interactions with my husband. I kept thinking, "He is on the verge of being cussed out, again. I don't care to give God honor, I'd rather give Don a piece of my mind." While she kept on praying, I became irritated.

After I got off the phone, I was mad at Mimi because she did not pray for God to get me out of my mess. She did not pray for God to open a door for me to walk out of his life. I decided right then and there that I would never pray with her again.

As life would have it, Mimi and I continued to communicate in the chat room numerous times during the week, and I eventually found out she also lived in my state. When we finally met, she asked me if she could pray for my marriage once again. In my mind, I was disgusted. Did she not hear how miserable I was? Why was Mimi still praying for me to be strong in my marriage? She even had the nerve to suggest that I pray for my marriage to have life in it once again.

I had no idea what that meant, but she prayed for the life of my marriage anyway. This was something I did not think to do for my marriage. I only knew to pray for people. After she was through praying, I will admit that I felt a teeny tiny hint of enthusiasm about my marriage. She gave me a few Scriptures to read daily to build up my faith. She told me that God only had good things in store for me and that He had a plan for my life. I finally had a sliver of hope that things would get better.

Let me pause here and say, in the 17 years that I have been married, I witnessed my marriage do a complete 180. Has it been rough? Absolutely. Were there days I wanted a divorce? Yes, plenty!

Were there days I wanted to call those beautiful men from the movie, Posse, to scoop me up, throw me on the back of their horses, and ride me off into the sunset? Heck yeah! But the one thing that kept me hanging in there was my couch time with Jesus. I spent more time on His couch during the early years of my marriage than I ever had in my entire life combined.

There were many nights I spent in my bedroom closet crying my eyes out with a towel in my mouth so my husband would not hear me. I prayed for hours that he would change and love me once again. I told God that I did not sign up for this. We were now expecting our first baby, but we could not even bear being in the same room together. How did this happen?

There was one night when Don acted like a wild banshee, cussing and fussing about something irrelevant. I stood there looking at this person that I loved and wondered, "Where is the awesome and super loving man I married?" You know, the one who used to visit my job all the time to shower me with cheap gifts. Remember that guy?

A few hours after that episode, that guy was tucked comfortably in bed, slumbering peacefully like a newborn babe. I was so angry at him that I could not sleep. That night, I wanted to leave him before he woke up. I was pregnant and on bedrest, so you know I would not get far.

I was disgusted that he was now asleep and I was stuck tossing and turning all night. I decided to pour a big bowl of ice-cold water on him while he slept. I know that was not the right thing to do, but at the time, it was the only thing I could do to hurt him back. I could not believe that my resentment at that point was so strong, that I wanted to hurt the man I loved.

Needless to say, Don woke up in utter shock. He could not believe his pregnant wife had the nerve to do this to him. Can you believe he said I was crazy? Really?!

During all of that, I began to feel in my heart that something was wrong with Don, but I had no idea what it was. My couch time with Jesus was the only thing I had to keep me from losing my mind when I knew my marriage was in trouble. So many times, I spent that time asking God to reveal to me what was going on with my husband.

Years later, God showed me that the issue was not me at all. I was so relieved but disappointed at the same time. I was disappointed because He showed me that even though the issue was not me, I had equally contributed to the drama in my marriage.

How could this be? Why did sweet, nice, little me get stuck with this guy who could be loving one minute and then cut me with the most hurtful words the next minute? I heard God quietly say to me, "Remember when you were dating him and you heard a voice say 'This is your husband?' This is the reason why. I told you to pray for Donald Barnett but you quit when things between you two got tough. You are so focused on complaining. Get over it. I'll take care of you but I need you to do your part—pray for him." Wow! Talk about a kick in the behind.

There were plenty of times when I was so fed up with Don that looking at him made me sick to my stomach. In those moments, God would often remind me to pray for my husband. I remember several years ago, a woman I admired suggested that I put oil on Don while he slept. She said it was a way to pray for him without him knowing and a way for me to connect with God.

He would wake up and think that I was giving him a massage and that this was "the sign" but in reality, I was praying for him. Disclaimer: the prayer rub will spark some things in him and in you, so be ready to give into that. In my personal opinion, I found that giving into these feelings that "arise," helps to seal the prayers. I still rub oil on him and pray over him in the middle of the night.

Through prayer, I was able to grow from feelings of anger toward my husband to actual feelings of empathy for him. God eventually showed me Don needed counseling for his feelings toward his mother. I clearly heard in my heart that my husband needed a stubborn woman like me to pray for him and to stay by his side. I vividly remember him saying that I was going to leave him like everyone else and no matter how much I told him I was not going anywhere, he could not receive it. He had become my assignment and taking care of him became my ministry.

There were days that he was so depressed that he was barely functioning. All I could do was crawl in the bed, lay beside him and pray. He could not hear his wife, "Tanya" speaking to him, but deep down inside, I knew I was speaking God's Word and life to his spirit. On other days, I would read Scripture to him while he laid in bed paralyzed with heaviness.

It came to a point where I also knew that he needed help I could not provide, so I continued to suggest counseling. Whenever I brought up counseling, you would have thought I was demanding that he run across a bed of hot coals with no shoes on. As he continued to refuse to go, I continued to pray that he would change his mind.

Mimi came into agreement with me, and she prayed for me to be strong and not give up. For years, we prayed with each other daily. We prayed for our husbands, marriages, finances, children, and even relationships with family members. I know that God heard us back then. It took years for me to see the results of those prayers, but the keys were persistence and consistency. I refused to give up on Donald Barnett.

Eventually, my prayers would be answered when God opened Don's eyes to accept my advice about attending a counseling session to deal with his anger. His stipulation was that I had to attend it with him because he said, "Little Miss Perfect, you have issues too."

When we initially went to counseling, Don would leave the sessions upset. He did not like the fact that I was honest with the counselor. He felt that I was making him look bad. In reality, I was sharing what was going on because I was hoping we could work through our issues. I wanted peace to return to our home. After a while, I couldn't handle Don being mad about the information I was sharing, so we stopped going to the sessions.

During my prayer time, I used to ask God to help me love my husband more and to see him as a person who had no examples of a good marriage. This changed the way I heard Don's ugly words. I no longer took them personally. Once I changed my perspective about why he was acting that way, his words no longer had the power to hurt me.

I asked God to help me be the wife he needed and to show me what I could do to lessen his burden until he could go to God himself. Initially, I did not want to do the things that I were being challenged to do, but I knew deep down in my heart that I was supposed to be married to Don. Knowing that, I was assured that God would give me the strength to weather the storms. Believe me, I am still praying, and God is still answering.

I know I have plenty areas in my life for more growth and maturity and I can say, emphatically, that I am not perfect. However, I no longer get so angry that I want to get away from Don by hopping on a private jet to the Fiji Islands to sip on mimosas, while munching on carrot cake and reading books all day. (Sounds delightful, doesn't it?)

I now pray when I sense something is not right with my husband. I have seen that when I pray for and love Donald Barnett unconditionally, his attitude changes, and he usually apologizes to me when he hurts my feelings. I notice that I, too, am now apologizing more often.

We also learned that we need to take the time to talk to each other. We give each other permission to be brutally honest about what is bothering us so we can deal with it and move on. There have been times where we've had to choose to agree to disagree, whereas, in the past, we both would not have budged off our positions and the need to be right. That type of behavior always led to ugly arguments, lots of silent treatments and no sex.

In prayer, God has shown me that the behavior we displayed was downright childish and that we were acting like two-year-olds. Looking back, we were actually having adult temper tantrums because we could not get our way. Making matters worse, we did this in front of our children.

Thank God, a few years later, another marriage counselor suggested that we stop this destructive behavior. That was the best advice we were ever given.

We both agreed and made a conscious effort to not argue in front of the kids.

When I feel an argument brewing, I quickly ask my husband to go to the "Zen Zone" to talk. We discuss the issue and when the conversation has concluded, we usually make up—which is the best part. We also take walks when we both get home from work and on weekends. There have been times when we would break out in prayer while walking. If someone told me 16 ½ years ago we would be as close as we are now, I would have told them they were insane.

The best testimony I can share with you of prayer working, was during a time when Gabi visited us a few months after moving out. She commented that she was shocked that daddy and I did not argue during her weekend visit. She asked what was going on with us. At the time, I had no answer for her question. I was in shock that she saw a difference.

Her question revealed to me that our kids really were and still are watching us. Don and I prayed that evening and asked God to forgive us for all those years we argued in front of the children. I believe He will remove those memories from our kids' minds to ensure they have loving marriages when their time comes.

So, sister girl, be encouraged. Don't give up! Fight for your marriage understanding that most issues in your marriage will take prayer to overcome them. I can't say it any plainer than that. Find a girlfriend who will pray with you and for you in your weakest moments.

Having a prayer partner was a lifesaver for me since I needed someone who would be honest with me about how I was wrong or to advise me on what I could do better. I also needed someone who would always point me back to God when I was ready to throw in the towel instead of being patient and waiting on God's promises regarding my marriage.

Reflection

• Do you pray or have "couch time" with Jesus? If you do pray, what does your prayer life look like?

_____

_____

_____

• What can you do to improve your prayer life?

_____

_____

_____

• What specific things can you intentionally pray about for your fiancé/husband?

_____

_____

_____

• If you do not pray, read the prayers in this book with conviction until they become your reality.

• If you do not have a prayer partner, ask God to bring one into your life. Ask for a prayer partner who will encourage you and be honest with you even when you are wrong. Pray that she will hold you accountable to make positive changes in your life.

Prayer

Father, I thank you for the gift of prayer. It is my way of speaking directly to you. I am thankful that I can come to you whenever and wherever I want: morning, afternoon or night.

Forgive me for those times when I did not come to you but tried to fix things myself. Remind me to bring all of my concerns to you. Open my eyes and heart to areas in my life and in my marriage where I need to focus my prayers. Help me intentionally pray for _____ daily as we navigate this marriage journey together.

Give me the wisdom to manage my time more effectively in order to come to you daily. Thank you for answering my prayers in the past. I thank you for answering my prayers today and in the future. Thank you for providing the things we need to have a healthy, successful, and love filled marriage.
In Jesus' name, Amen.

Thoughts/Prayer Requests

4 Patience: Who Has Time For That?

We can rejoice, too, when we run into problems and trials, for we know that they are good for us—they help us learn to be patient. And patience develops strength of character in us and helps us trust God more each time we use it until finally, our hope and faith are strong and steady. —Romans 5:3 & 4 (TLB)

As I was writing this book, I reflected so many times over my entire life and the many choices I made that did not have positive outcomes. I realized and can finally admit that I have never been a patient person. When I wanted something, I just went after it with reckless abandonment. Most times, I never thought my decisions through or weighed any options before making choices. I never considered any consequences prior to making decisions.

When I was in second grade, I wanted to learn how to ride my bike because all of my friends already could. My dad was away on travel, so I asked my friend Shelly's dad to teach me. Before the day was over, I joined the ranks of two-wheeler graduates in Happy Acres Elementary School.

I had no idea this would be a major disappointment for my dad since I did not go to him first. My rush to ride my bike robbed him of the opportunity to teach me, his first born child, to ride a bike.

Fast forward fifteen years—I joined the Air Force in 1993. I signed up to be a medical technician and was extremely excited that I would be working in a hospital. After boot camp, I went to technical school and then to clinical training, where I received hands on training for my job.

During this training, I fell in love with Labor and Delivery. I had an extra strong desire to work there after I was told no one ever gets that as their first assignment coming out of "Clinicals." I was determined that I would be the first person who would get assigned there.

I worked extremely hard to be seen by Labor and Delivery management during my training. I put in my request to be assigned to work in Labor and Delivery (L&D). At the completion of my training, the Labor and Delivery supervisor approved me to work there. I was so elated to have proved all the naysayers wrong.

That excitement wore off the minute I got my first schedule. What I did not know was that L&D staff worked twelve-hour shifts. I was put on the night shift since I was the "new girl," which meant I was scheduled to work three nights on, two nights off. Immediately, this assignment became a complete nightmare.

Since I was a single mom, I had to hire a babysitter for the night shift, so I could go to work and another one for during the day, so I could sleep. When I realized I did not have enough money to have two babysitters, I got rid of the daytime sitter. I figured that I would just sleep whenever I got Gabi settled down with Cheerios, two full sippy cups and her favorite Barney VHS tapes.

I soon realized how much damage a twenty-month-old toddler could inflict while running around an apartment unsupervised. Can you say, "Bye-bye $250 security deposit?" I could go on and on about all the hasty decisions I made without any thought and without any patience.

In the midst of reflecting on the days and months leading up to our wedding day, I came to the realization that the majority of human beings do not receive any real advice pertaining to marriage. I mean—None! Zero! Zilch! Nada!

Prior to our glorious wedding day, we are not taught how to endure the bad and ugly times. If you were anything like me, you probably went into your marriage with visions of perpetual loving, wedded bliss.

I was taught by my parents to work hard, to be honest, and to show up early in order for good things to happen for you. Who could go wrong by adhering to those wonderful words of wisdom?

Well, I do not remember hearing them say that I should exercise patience and carefully weigh any choices I was about to make before I made them. I also do not recall them saying that sometimes, I would have to just wait for certain things to work out in my favor.

I was never told that no matter how hard you work to make your marriage better, you will have to wait for God to do things in His timing. Um, yeah, I did not get that information in Marriage 101, and I definitely did not receive it in premarital counseling.

So, you can imagine my initial reaction when all hell broke loose in my marriage. I literally wanted to do a FloJo out the back door and never come back. I was not mentally or emotionally prepared to endure the ugliness that transpired. I was never taught to patiently wait on God to do His thing to improve my marriage. No one prepared me for the "realness" of marriage. Instead of lions, tigers and bears, you wake up to bills, kids, and fights, oh my!

I only saw my parents "live" marriage, but they never taught me how to do the "work" of marriage. I am not blaming my parents at all for the issues I had in my marriage or for my inability to handle them at the beginning. I am merely stating that people do not seem to share the real stuff that marriage consists of with young people before they get married.

Don and I had serious issues at the beginning of our marriage. I can look back on them and laugh now, but at the time, they were no laughing matter.

We argued about the most mundane things. We argued over whether to use Tide detergent (him) or another less expensive one (me). We were on one income at the time, so I made an executive decision that the cheaper one was friendlier to our budget.

One day, I decided to buy the less expensive detergent and pour it into the Tide bottle without Don knowing about it. I did this for years, and he never suspected a thing. I did not tell him about this until years later and he was dumbfounded that I kept him in the dark about this for years. After that, you know, we only purchased the less expensive brands. That was genius if I do not mind saying so myself.

Month four into our marriage, I found out I was pregnant. Don was so happy and showered me with so much love and affection. I was like, "Wow, he loves me again!" He catered to all my nutritional needs since I was nauseous all the time. He went out to buy Chipwich ice cream sandwiches from 7-11 and Welch's grape popsicles from the grocery store almost nightly. Those were the only items I could eat without feeling sick.

Don also purchased six-packs of ginger ale and boxes of saltine crackers to settle my queasy stomach and to ensure that I would have something to snack on at night. Soon, he would bring five to ten Chipwiches home at a time because those late night runs were wearing him down.

I remember when there was a snowstorm, we ran out of Chipwich sandwiches. That was a serious situation. You know, I had to have my Chipwiches in order to survive. Don decided he was going to brave the elements to ensure he did not have to hear my mouth. He dressed warmly and he and a friend walked to the 7-11 to buy them for me. Hey, I had to eat! I was growing a human being while he was watching Sports Center.

Because I was pregnant, I convinced myself that I was now living in true "holy matrimony" with my husband. Boy, was I fooling myself. Before I knew it, I was unknowingly pissing him off again because I did or did not do something he wanted. The majority of the time, I had no idea what I had done to offend my husband. This would then cause me to become angry and offended by everything he did. This was our existence.

Remember the ice-cold-water-on-his-head-as-he-slept incident? Well, that was on the same day that he trudged through a snowstorm to get my food. That's crazy, I know. I decided to pour the water on him as a direct result of me being fed up with his unkind words earlier that day. This day was different though, I decided I was going to fight back.

The next thing I knew, he was screaming about how crazy I was, that he hated me and that he was leaving. He actually ran downstairs to get his toolbox from the garage. All the while, he continued to cuss and scream at me that he never should have married me.

When he came back upstairs, he had the toolbox in his hand and then proceeded to take our bed apart. For a few minutes, I watched, in awe and disbelief. Once my brain processed what was going on, I started to chuckle, which took him to the highest level of pissed-offness. I was standing there in disbelief, with my hands folded over my growing belly thinking, "This fool has lost his freaking mind. Is he really taking apart our bed in the middle of the night?"

By the time he was done, he was so disgusted with me, he could not even speak. He yelled for his friend to help him drag the mattress down the stairs. After they got the mattress downstairs, he attempted to carry it out of the house. I could hear his friend telling him to calm down and that everything would be okay. He shouted up the stairs that I would be hearing from his lawyer (mind you, we were too poor to afford one) and that he would be getting full custody of the baby I was carrying.

Once I finally decided I had had enough of his foolish behavior, I went into the guest bedroom and fell fast asleep. After all, I was growing a baby and needed my beauty sleep. Mr. "I'm Calling My Lawyer," eventually fell asleep on the sofa. He finally put the bed back together a few days later and slept in our room— alone.

I, on the other hand, continued to sleep in the guest bedroom without a care in the world except for the baby and Gabi. I made up my mind that once this baby was born, I was finally out of this stinking marriage and that I would be moving in with somebody, anybody. I did not have a clue who that somebody was, I just knew I was out the door, never to return. In my mind, I saw myself giving Don the peace sign and a few other signs, as I walked away hollering, "Hasta la vista, baby!"

When I tell you we had some crazy days, you've got to believe that I am not making this stuff up. Don and I had some of the most stupid arguments. We even argued over beans and hot dogs. Do you hear me? Beans and dogs!

We couldn't agree if toilet paper should be put on the roll with the sheets hanging over or under? Who does that you might ask? We did, that's who.

We were ridiculously uncivilized towards each other, all the while heading to prenatal appointments and putting up a front for other people, especially my parents. We pretended that we were in love but in reality, it was anything but that.

To be perfectly honest, I only had sex with Don so I would not have to hear his mouth about not getting any, not because I loved him. I don't think I loved my husband at the time; I think I was more so tolerating him. Besides, I was a new bride, a stay-at-home mom and had absolutely nowhere to go. I couldn't let my parents know how miserable I was or my dad would have "dealt with" Don in a not so nice way.

During this time, the only two people I could share my feelings with were Mimi and my childhood friend, Shelly. They continued to encourage me by stating that one day we would get it together and that things would improve. I just could not see how this was possible. The man I loved was acting like a complete jerk all while I was carrying his baby.

Around this time, I made a decision to get serious about prayer and my relationship with God. He actually was the only person who would listen to me morning, noon and during so many middle of the nights. I have to be honest and say that I was no Mother Theresa at the time, but I did know that I had to lean on God in order to handle all the negative energy.

Also during this time, my terrible nausea escalated to an excruciating case of morning sickness. On top of the three-ring circus that my marriage had become, I started puking my guts out 24/7. Between vomiting and crying, I tried to pray. I was praying for a break from all the vomiting and I was praying for a break from Donald Barnett, who now smelled like sour pickles to me. I cried all the time. I thought to myself, that I would not survive 40 more minutes of this pregnancy, let alone 40 weeks.

Because of the morning sickness, the smell of food constantly sent me running to the bathroom or lying on the sofa with all the windows open to get fresh air. I only found relief when I was outdoors. Eventually, I found myself relegated to spending evenings outside on the porch while Don cooked dinner. Let's just say, I did not like this arrangement so I did everything I could to criticize him.

Remember the beans and hot dogs? Well, that is where those arguments came from. Don, who was new to dinner duty, felt this was an appropriate dinner since that's what he ate growing up. I, on the other hand, was used to a meat, a starch, a vegetable and Kool-Aid if you were good, at dinnertime. In my home, beans and hot dogs were lunch food, not dinner food.

We even argued about deodorant, toothpaste, and toilet paper brands. Oh, and we argued about how to prepare spaghetti; sauce mixed in the noodles or on top of the noodles. Since Don was a one-pot meal guy, I, much to my dismay, was stuck eating spaghetti with the noodles mixed in. After all, it is impossible to dictate what was on the dinner menu while sitting outside.

This arrangement annoyed me to no end. I did not want to give up having things done the way I thought they should be. I could not process how two people, who were once madly in love with each other, could no longer agree on anything, to include spaghetti preparation.

Eventually, the stress from arguing all the time sent me to the hospital with Braxton Hicks contractions at the twentieth week of my pregnancy. I visited Labor and Delivery three different times in premature labor before my doctor finally admitted me for an entire week. It was truly a miserable existence. I was not the poster child of pregnancy. Quite the contrary, I was the "Everything that could go wrong in pregnancy, you name it" poster child.

While I was confined to the hospital with my bed in Trendelenburg (basically upside down so the baby would not put pressure on my cervix) and drugged to the max to keep me from contracting, my hubby was once again in that place of helplessness.

This time, he was worried about two lives: mine and that of our unborn baby, his first child. To make matters worse, Don had to go to work every day and take care of Gabi by himself; something he had never done before. This was about the most stressful thing either of us had experienced so far since we said, "I do".

When I finally had enough energy to think clearly, I asked Don to bring a CD player to the hospital so I could at least have some music to listen to. I loved the Men of Standard song, "Yet Will I Trust in Him," so I had him set that song on repeat for days. That song was the only prayer I could utter because of the drugs I was given.

The drugs were so strong that I was literally in and out of consciousness for hours at a time. When my husband came to sit with me after working a full day, we would pray for the life of our baby. We asked God to spare the baby's life and to bring us closer in the midst of this craziness.

That was the first time we truly prayed together for a common thing. All we had at that point was prayer and each other. We also had to be patient and trust God to keep this baby from being born prematurely.

After being discharged from the hospital, I was sent home on bedrest with a medical IV pump that gave me continuous medicine to relax my uterus so it would not contract. The medicines did not work and I continued to have contractions the remainder of my pregnancy. I was also assigned a home healthcare nurse who visited me weekly to change my IV tubing and ask me questions about my week.

I had nothing but endless hours of TV watching, sleeping and waiting for the weeks to go by. It was during that time that Mimi and I began to talk and pray daily. We discussed our marriages, our hopes and dreams and the babies we both were carrying at that time. She suggested I take advantage of this time to attempt to get quiet so I could hear from God. Hey, I had nothing but time on my hands, so I did just that.

In my quiet time, I contemplated my life and what I wanted for my growing family. During that time, God showed me that I was selfish, immature and a bully. He also exposed that because I was so independent, I did not allow Don to be a man nor a husband. Looking back, I ordered him around a lot. When he did not do what I wanted him to do at the exact moment I wanted it done, I would be mean to him. I was a "real" terrible wife but I felt justified in my behavior.

As I wrote this paragraph, I was reflecting on that time so many years ago. I have come to realize that the reason I acted that way towards Don was because I was angry and resentful that I had to depend on my husband. That was painful for me because I was so accustomed to taking care of myself and Gabi for seven years. I was taught to be a strong woman who could take care of herself. I wanted to remain independent; that's all I knew. I didn't know, that in marriage, you are interdependent.

Even though I received this revelation about myself, I continued to remain a stubborn bully and quite immature. I utterly shut down towards Don. I found myself going through the marriage motions without even remotely putting any of my heart into them. Quite frankly, I decided to focus my time and energy on my kids only. I, ultimately, neglected my marriage, my appearance and my health, too.

I now know I was also suffering from mild depression. I gained weight and just did not care about my marriage. Don partied all the time with his fraternity brothers, drank his sorrows away and also slipped into depression. We were in a nasty cycle that was not going anywhere.

When I did choose to give God my attention, I knew I heard Him speaking to me about my mindset and behaviors. However, I chose to continue in those behaviors because I felt like I was the victim in the marriage.

During the first two years of my marriage, I changed. Gone was the blushing bride, who was madly in love with the man of her dreams. I had become a stubborn, bitter and impatient wife with no regard for anyone but myself and kids. My mindset was straight self-preservation and the survival of my baby along with feeling like I was in control.

While on bedrest, I was at the mercy of waiting on Don to do things for me. Because of my need for control, I would insist my husband do the laundry on Thursdays because that was the day we washed clothes in my home growing up. When he did not follow through, I would get off the sofa and drag the laundry from upstairs to downstairs, wash, sort and fold it, and then take it back upstairs before he got home from work.

I did things like this often in an attempt to make him feel bad but because he was stubborn too, it didn't work. I would verbally compare him to my dad and tell him all the things my dad did for us and my mom when we were growing up. I was hoping that by doing this, he would feel guilty and step up to his responsibilities. I was clueless to the fact that he had no idea how to do some of those things. He never had to do them or was never taught to do those things for a household or family.

The straw that broke the camel's back was when my dad came to visit us. I knew my dad was coming to visit, so I decided to cut our overgrown grass; while on bedrest. That was not a typo: Yes, girl, I was on bedrest. My dad commented on how nice the grass looked and that he was proud of Don for making the yard look nice. This angered me. I decided I would use this opportunity to make myself look good and to make Don look bad.

I proudly boasted to my dad that I, in fact, cut the grass, not Don. You could not tell me anything in that moment. I'm sure my chest was just as puffed up and out like my big belly. I just knew my dad would be angry at Don for not cutting the grass.

Needless to say, that backfired. My dad went off on me. He told me how disappointed he was in my behavior. He couldn't understand how I could blatantly put my pregnancy in danger because the stupid grass was not cut. He told me nothing in life was that serious.

When Don got home from work, he assumed my dad had cut the grass. Imagine his surprise when he found out it was me. He was beyond angry. He cursed me out for taking such a crazy risk just because I wanted the grass cut. My rationale was that I was tired of asking him to do stuff around the house only for him to blow me off. That was my way to get even with him.

He told me that he could not forgive the fact that I threw him under the bus in front of my dad. I saw nothing wrong with it since, in my mind, he should have already cut the grass, so I didn't have to.

We already had several arguments surrounding yardwork and the grass being cut. Don would purposefully allow it to get high to irritate me. It was embarrassing to me to be the only yard on our street with high grass.

You would think all of this drama would have made us change our ways. Well, it did not. We were so focused on having our own ways, that the health of our baby was in jeopardy, and we weren't even cognizant of it. Needless to say, Don and I kept arguing about dumb things.

I finally got to the point where I was so sick of having morning sickness, that I wanted the pregnancy to hurry up and be over. Before I knew it, I was back in the hospital at the 24th week of my pregnancy. That time, I was contracting so badly that I felt like I was in full blown labor.

My doctor was called and thankfully, she came to the hospital immediately. She was so fed up with our shenanigans that she yelled at me with absolutely no sympathy. Dr. Fleming was not a woman you crossed. She did not mix her words and she said what she meant with no regard to how you received it.

She flat out told me that I was going to deliver a preemie, and that the odds of its survival were not good. She told us that even if this baby survived, it would have all sorts of medical and health issues due to being born so early.

Having previously been a L&D technician in the military and again at Prince George's Hospital Center, I was devastated. As an L&D technician, I assisted with deliveries where most of the preemies, who were born that early, died. I was responsible for their paperwork, their final goodbyes to their mommies and then transporting them to the morgue. I was mortified.

Once again, I was admitted to the hospital and given more drugs to stop the contractions. That time, instead of camping out beside my hospital bed, Don found himself once again having to go to work every day.

He was devastated that he could not stay at the hospital with me. He came to the hospital after work but could only stay an hour because of the visiting hours and the fact that he had to get Gabi from the neighbors and take care of her.

During the time he sat with me, we would literally sit there looking at each other terrified. The baby monitor produced unending waves of contractions. I was in so much pain, that I knew I was in labor. I was afraid. A nurse checked my cervix and told us that it was indeed opening and that I had progressed to two centimeters. She apologized profusely, since we knew each other from working together in this same hospital.

An L&D technician came in the room and created baby bands as I was being prepped for the delivery of my baby. I cried out to God to save my unborn child. My husband grabbed my hand, and we prayed with all the strength we had. We declared that this baby would not be born prematurely.

The neonatal and pediatric staffs came in to talk to us about what to expect once the baby was born. I was given a shot of the steroid Surfactant, to mature the baby's lungs in hopes that it would prevent its lungs from collapsing at birth.

The radiology team also came in to perform a last minute sonogram. At that moment, we found out the baby was a girl. We decided to pray using her name, Donielle Jahnaé Barnett. We prayed earnestly for God to reduce the contractions and to stop my labor.

Within twenty-four hours of all the preparation for the delivery of my baby, all the contractions subsided and my labor ceased. The medical team was amazed and so were we. Even though we knew it was the direct result of concentrated and specific prayer, we were still shocked to see that our praying worked.

We continued this prayer for several more days. A few days later, I was discharged with doctor's orders to rest completely. However, true to form, we were back to arguing and fussing with each other just a few days later.

I had several more hospital visits for premature labor throughout that pregnancy. My home health care nurse, who was now like an aunt, continued to encourage me about carrying the pregnancy out to full term. She allowed me to share my concerns with her about the stress of my trying marriage and my desire to not deliver this baby early. She eventually taught me how to change my IV tubing and how to give myself the medicines for the remainder of my pregnancy. Those medicines reduced my contractions, but they never stopped them.

A few weeks before my due date, I had a terrible cough that would not go away after several doctor's appointments. I decided to have Don take me to the emergency room for another opinion. The x-rays showed I had a terrible case of pneumonia so I was again, admitted to L&D. The on-call doctor chose to hospitalize me in order to give me IV antibiotics. They called Dr. Fleming, who decided to induce my labor. I think she was just as tired as we were of all the hospitalizations.

I experienced three days of intense, mind-blowing labor that was topped off with a 105 degree fever. By the morning of the third day, I knew something was wrong. I asked the medical staff to call Dr. Fleming because I was experiencing increasing pain that was not relieved by the Epidural. The moment she saw me, she rushed me to the operating room.

Donielle was born at 37 weeks via an emergency Caesarean section. After I was resting comfortably in my room, Dr. Fleming told me that she was glad I had them call her. My placenta was detaching from my uterus (an abruption) due to being in labor for three days and that it created a life or death situation for me and the baby. I thank God every day for the ability to hear His voice.

Once we were settled at home, life was great again. Don and I were in love with each other and this new baby. Gabi enjoyed being a big sister and helping with the baby too. Six weeks after Donielle was born, Don left for boot camp.

For the ten months he was in boot camp and then technical training school, I finally had a peaceful home. We seemed to be getting along with him in Florida and me still in Maryland with the girls. I enjoyed the time Don was away and I believed, at the time, that we were making progress in our marriage.

At the end of his training, Don received orders to be stationed at a base in Germany. Initially, things were great, and we were able to travel around the country on his off days.

About six months later, much to my dismay, I found out I was pregnant again. This was not part of our plan. The plan was to wait until Donielle was in kindergarten; she was only 18 months old. To top it all off, a few weeks later, the evil nausea was back and I was miserable once again.

On a peaceful and relaxing evening, I felt a warm gush of fluid flow down my leg. I started screaming at the top of my lungs because I was only around 15 weeks pregnant. My husband ran into the bedroom to find me standing in a puddle of amniotic fluid. He asked me why I "peed" on the floor and why it had me crying hysterically.

Once I told him what it was, he delicately picked me up and gently placed me on the bed. This time, he was reassuring me that things would be okay. I was beyond terrified and to make matters worse, I had just taken out half of my braids.

Sidebar: My African American sisters totally understand that you do not go out of the house when you only have half of your braids taken out.

Don called a friend of ours, who lived a couple of apartment buildings away from us, to take our daughters to their home so we could go to the hospital. When our friend walked into our bedroom to check on me, he immediately laid hands on me and prayed. As he prayed, I slowly felt myself begin to calm down. The three of us stood there praying while we waited for the ambulance.

Once it arrived, we gave the girls to him. I was loaded into the ambulance and had to ride by myself while Don followed behind in our car. I felt so alone and trapped during that long ride to the hospital. All I could do was beg God to not take this baby at 15 weeks. This was the second scariest event in my entire life.

When I arrived at the hospital, they whisked me to L&D since they believed my delivery of this baby was imminent. We had a major problem though, the on-duty staff only spoke German. They could not understand us, and we could not understand them. It was like something out of a comedy movie, only it was not funny.

We did the best we could with the language barrier but we were having minimal success with hand gestures. Finally, the hospital found someone who spoke very little English but it was enough for us to convey our message and vice versa.

The L&D staff called the radiology department to perform a sonogram to see how much amniotic fluid I had lost. My only memory of the radiology exam was of the translator saying that the sonogram showed I had a small amount of fluid. With very little emotion, the on-call doctor discharged me saying that once I miscarried at home, they wanted me to bring my fetus back in a margarine container.

I do not know what happened in that moment, but I immediately prayed out loud with Don joining in. We started shouting God's words. Don kept telling them we were not delivering a fetus at home but that our baby would be born at 40 weeks. I know the doctor thought we were crazy and he probably did not understand what we were saying, but we didn't care.

On our ride home, we continued praying and believing God would refill my uterus with the fluid this baby needed to survive. We were exhausted by the time we returned home, and I believe the wait to see if we could schedule a doctor's appointment was just as draining. During the wee hours of that morning, I had to once again wait on God.

With the help of an interpreter on base, I was able to contact the on-call doctor. He told us he was going to notify my doctor that I was coming in for an appointment when the office opened.

At the appointment, a radiology technician performed a sonogram. She was very quiet, which made us very nervous. She left the room and a few minutes later, returned with the radiologist. He performed yet, another sonogram. They had shocked looks on their faces but we had no idea why. They left the room without a word to us. Don and I sat there trying to keep our minds thinking positive thoughts, but we were scared.

When they returned, they told me to get dressed and to go back upstairs to see my doctor. We were met by my doctor's nurse who led us into a room and asked me to get undressed. My doctor finally came in the exam room and said that the sonogram showed that my uterus was full of amniotic fluid. He did a quick exam of me and said the baby was fine. He sent me home on strict bedrest for the remainder of the pregnancy.

I had several more visits to my German doctor and another hospitalization for premature labor before I was eventually admitted to the hospital. This time, I was experiencing an excruciating pain in my side along with contractions. My doctor had no idea where the pain was coming from so he opted to deliver the baby early. Jakim Déjon was born by C-section at 34 weeks and weighed four pounds. He was admitted to the NICU for 10 days.

During those 10 days I remained in the hospital, I cried and I prayed. I prayed and cried! I experienced a combination of emotional, physical and mental pain that was so severe, I literally thought I was going to lose my mind.

I was in physical pain from the C-section incision, enormous hemorrhoids, and engorged breasts full of milk. To add insult to injury, the NICU was three floors away from L&D due to reconstruction. The first two days they wheeled me down to see Jakim but the other eight days, I had to catch the elevator and walk.

I was in constant emotional pain because of guilt. I complained the entire pregnancy, and I wanted it over because of the morning sickness. Because my baby was in the NICU, I felt it was my fault. I was also stuck in a German hospital where no one spoke English. The hospital staff was trying their best to explain what was going on with the baby, but we just could not communicate.

I was in mental pain due to the exhaustion of being married to Donald Barnett. Instead of being a happy mommy of a beautiful baby boy, my husband made me feel guilty every time we talked. He was angry with me because he felt my complaining words caused the baby to be born early.

I begged God to give me a break. God told me to be patient. You know I let Him know I didn't have time for that. Right there in the NICU, while nursing my son, I plotted and planned how I was going to justify flying back to the United States with my new baby and my two daughters.

I knew my parents would take me, the girls and their first grandson in with no questions asked. I decided I would wait until my six-weeks were over before I ran my plan by them.

A few weeks later, God, in His infinite wisdom and His constant sense of humor, worked our situation out where our family, to include Donald Barnett, was to be flown back to the United States. I was not happy. I wanted to leave Don in Germany.

Don received a compassionate reassignment through his Army Command because Jakim was very sick all the time and the German doctors did not know what was wrong with him. He had been in the hospital numerous times, and I was not happy that no one could figure out what was wrong with him.

We received orders for Fort Meade Army Base in Maryland, which enabled us to live with my parents. The day after we arrived, I took Jakim to Walter Reed Army Medical Center for the care he needed. That was not part of my plan but obviously, God knew what he was doing. Jakim received first class care and his health improved immediately.

At my parent's house, Don and I argued worse than before due to the stress of living with my folks. I told Jesus that I was officially done and could not be married to this man another minute.

It was at that time when Don began to say to me that if I felt that he made me so miserable, then I should find a man who can give me what I needed. This became his go-to line every time we had an argument or if I asked him to value me. Boy, did this come back to haunt us a few years later.

While living at my parent's house, I got a job in Howard University's emergency room. One weekend, after two long 12-hour shifts, Don was waiting for me with another complaint about our living arrangements.

We were in the process of attempting to buy our first home but every contract we put in was outbid by thousands of dollars. It felt like we would be stuck living with my parents forever. Well, that night I had enough of his complaining. I told him that if he was so miserable, that he could pack his bags and move out. I also let him know the kids and I were staying with my folks.

I told him the discussion was over and that I needed to get to bed. After shedding a few tears in the shower, I slipped in bed, picked up my Bible and told God that He had to give me a sign that I was to stay with this man. At the time, I was making between $20-$35/hour, so I figured I could save up enough money to get my own place.

Wouldn't you know I stumbled upon 1 Peter 3:1-2 in The Living Bible? It read, "Wives, fit in with your husbands' plans; for then if they refuse to listen when you talk to them about the Lord, they will be won by your respectful, pure behavior. Your godly lives will speak to them better than any words." I had to reread that last verse a few times just to be sure those words were not a typo. I even read the footnotes at the bottom of my Bible to see if the words meant what I thought they meant.

It was during that season that God told me I had to change my mind and my way of doing things, if I wanted to experience change in my marriage. I actively fought God on changing. I could not understand why God was asking me to be the agent of change, but Don got a free pass to do as he darn well pleased. I complained to Him and asked Him why I had to be the one to forgive, while He let Don continue to be unkind to me. I told God this request just was not fair.

He showed me that the changes I so desperately desired, had to start with me surrendering my will to His. I finally understood my husband needed to have a living example of true love and sacrifice; something he had never experienced before.

God told me that I had to trust Him, to be patient and to allow the process to work. God used those verses to show me that I was supposed to stay with Don.

I finally wanted to change my attitude, my behavior and the way I loved my husband. I also longed for Don to change too. Little did I know how my conscious choice to change my ways, would not only change my life, but Donald Barnett's life too.

Reflection

• In what areas of your marriage do you find you lack patience? If you are engaged, what things do you notice that are a little annoying about your fiancé? Why?

_____

_____

_____

• What is one thing you can do today to help you begin to overcome your lack of patience in those areas?

_____

_____

_____

• How can making a choice to change how you respond to situations that try your patience, improve your relationships?

_____

_____

_____

Prayer

Lord, your Word says that Love is patient and Love is kind. Forgive me for not being patient and kind with _____. Help me be more like you. Give me the wisdom to pick my battles as you see them. Help me to be quiet when necessary because sometimes, I can make situations worse.

In the times you tell me to be quiet, open my ears to hear what you have to say to me regarding my own ways and how they negatively affect my relationships and marriage. Cleanse me of thoughts, attitudes and behaviors that are not like you.

Strengthen me to pray for my husband instead of tearing him down. Give me the wisdom to see how I can grow in love and patience for my husband.

Thank you for not treating me the way I have treated him. Forgive me for being inconsiderate and unloving to _____. Thank you for changing my heart to be more loving and more patient.
In Jesus' name, Amen.

Thoughts/Prayer Requests

_____

_____

_____

_____

_____

_____

_____

_____

_____

_____

_____

_____

_____

_____

_____

_____

_____

_____

5 Perspective: Getting My Mind Right

"We delight in the beauty of the butterfly, but rarely admit the changes it has gone through to achieve that beauty." —Maya Angelou

Have you ever watched an elapsed-time video of a caterpillar creating the chrysalis? The journey a caterpillar must take to become a beautiful butterfly is the most disturbing and disgusting thing I have ever witnessed. I actually covered my eyes numerous times as I watched countless YouTube videos of this transformation with my teenage son.

The caterpillar spends hours eating leaves in preparation for the next stage in its journey. When the time comes for the chrysalis stage, the caterpillar attaches to a tree upside down. Spoiler alert: it actually splits in half as it opens up to expose a chrysalis.

They completely die to their old selves and show no resemblance of what they used to be. No matter how grossed out I was by the videos, I was amazed by the transformation. It looked painful, labor intensive and time-consuming.

Caterpillars reside in the chrysalis for up to two weeks (patiently allowing the process of change to happen). While in the chrysalis, the caterpillar has a vital decision to make. It could: 1) decide the wait is too long, give up and die, 2) decide the wait is too long, break out before it is ready, and die, 3) decide to never come out for fear of the unknown and die, or 4) decide to trust the process, be patient and wait for the journey to come to an end. The choice to wait produces a brand new and glorious creature that was hidden deep down inside the caterpillar. Its perspective about the process determines its outcome.

Just like the caterpillar, I endured a labor intensive transformation. I had to change my perspective pertaining to my marriage in order to take positive actions to produce positive change. There still are times in my marriage when choosing to apologize to Don is uncomfortable. I know I have to do it regardless as an extension of God's grace and mercy. Hour-long conversations, with Don, were labor intensive but resulted in many compromises.

Endless hours of prayer were time consuming, but I know God heard every one of them. The caterpillar's metamorphosis is equivalent to the changes my marriage had to undergo during the last 17 years. The woman I am today is a completely different person from the one who said, "I do" to Donald Barnett on June 12, 1999.

Have you ever heard of the saying, "You can either see the glass as half empty or half full?" Well, during the early portion of my marriage, my marriage glass was constantly bone-dry like the Mojave Desert. I only recently chose to begin to see my marriage glass as completely full and running over, like Niagara Falls.

Once I decided to change my perspective on that age old saying, my life began to improve in so many areas, including my marriage. I had to persistently work on getting my mind right. I knew that if I continued to meditate on 1st Peter 3:2, God would do something. I had no idea what that something was going to look like, but I had just enough sense and faith to believe it.

God had his hands full with me. I needed major reconstructive surgery on my mind and heart to begin the process of loving my husband like I should. I had no idea that it was going to be a long and strenuous process. I thank God for the grace to continue in the process. Sometimes, stubborn people need more time to get it right. Trust me, I know. That was me.

Around the twelfth year of our marriage, I began home-schooling our two youngest children after discovering my third grade daughter was not reading on grade level. Honestly, attempting to home-school a third grader who read on a first grade level, while teaching a first grader who read on a fourth grade level, was extremely challenging. Just reading this makes me look back and wonder how I made it through those years.

During the first few weeks, I cried all the time, right along with my nine-year-old daughter. I would frequently call my husband at work to tell him I could not do this anymore. Doni wanted to go back to school, and I wanted to go back to working outside of my home. You know, "work a real job."

I asked God, "Why me? Why do I have to always be the one in this marriage who has to do things I don't want to?" Soon after that, I became envious of other moms who went to work outside the home. I measured my self-worth and value on what I saw other moms doing with their families. I wanted to be able to afford a family vacation, designer purses and yes, even the red-bottomed shoes.

Of course, I knew being home with my children was priceless. I also knew home-schooling my children was a necessary investment into their future. Even though I knew all of this, I hated where I was emotionally, spiritually and most of all, financially.

To compound all of that, my husband was stressed out about his job, which made our relationship ridiculously volatile. When he came home from work, I felt the need to dump the kids on him. I had been with them all day, along with my home day-care kids so I needed a break. I was also working on my Bachelor's Degree while trying to help my teenage daughter graduate from high school. I know, I was truly "doing the most."

Unbeknownst to me, when Don came home in the evening, he needed time alone to decompress from his stressful and deadline-driven job. All he wanted to do was watch television to relieve the stress from his work day. He did not want to hear me complaining about the kids or bills.

Not once did either of us attempt to accommodate each other's needs or even talk about them. We merely concentrated on relieving our stress in whatever capacity we could find: I ate food for comfort, and Don watched hours of television and hung out with friends basically every weekend.

There were numerous times during this period when we were pretty sure we were headed to divorce court. One night, we even sat on the side of the bed, weighed our options and came up with a plan to cohabitate until we could save enough money to go through a divorce. By the time our conversation was over, we came to the grim conclusion that we did not have the money to even submit the paperwork.

We laughed so hard at how ridiculous we sounded, that we finally decided that we might as well stay together. We rationalized that we were great business partners and great parents, but we were not great as husband and wife. We told each other what awesome qualities the other had to make someone else happy. The conversation then went from all the reasons why we should get a divorce to all the reasons why we should stay together as roommates.

A few months later, I met a lady named Mrs. Washington, and the words this lady shared with me changed my whole perspective on being a wife. At the time I met her, I was not only a home day-care provider but I was also a Mary Kay salesperson. (I was a Jill of all trades). I approached her in a store to give her my card and to offer her a free facial. Mrs. Washington asked me if I was married, and I told her that I was.

She proceeded to tell me that she had recently buried her husband of 40-plus years. She regretted that she neglected not only herself but how she also neglected him and her marriage for a long time. She shared how sick he was the last year of his life and how she had to care for him.

She told me that even though they could no longer be sexually intimate, she found that just lying beside him, rubbing his back and telling him what she loved about him became their most intimate moments. I felt her pain when she said how much she missed her husband.

With tears in her eyes, Mrs. Washington bluntly asked me why I was dressed in a frumpy manner. She commented on my baggy tee-shirt, mom jeans and flip flops. Mind you, I had never seen this woman before and this conversation was going on in the middle of the aisle of a store.

I explained to her that I was home with my kids and day-care kids all day and that this was what was comfortable for me to wear. I rattled off the laundry list of all the "stuff" I was doing and how I had no time for anything else. She looked me squarely in my eyes and said that she did not care about that.

She asked if that was what my husband came home to at the end of a hard day at work. Even though I was extremely annoyed by all her questions, I solemnly nodded my head. With much attitude, she told me to get some of that Mary Kay lip gloss I was trying to sell to her and put it on before my husband got home from work. She also instructed me to change into something cute that would catch my husband's eye.

She explained that my husband was most likely looking at cute, sexy women all day long at work and then had to go home to frumpy 'ole me. I never thought about that before. She equipped me with what I needed to get out of our 12-year slump: a perspective change.

The next day, I made sure I squeezed my size 16 body into my cutest size 14 outfit. Oh, and you know that I made sure my dark berry Mary Kay lip gloss was popping. I was determined to catch my husband's eye when he walked in the door. I heard Mrs. Washington's words replay in my mind, "Do you want him coming home to you and your homely self after looking at and working with sexiness all day long? You have the power to win your man's heart back."

She was right. When Don got home, he noticed me immediately. He was shocked at my appearance and asked me where I was going. I told him I had an appointment with him in the "Zen Zone." Need I say more? He could not wait for the day-care kids to leave for the evening and neither could I.

From that day forward, my husband has always come home to me looking ever so cute. I purposefully get dressed and at least wear lip-gloss on my days off. I also got rid of all t-shirts, shorts, and sweat pants I wore to bed and purchased cute "little" nightgowns. A few years ago, when menopause entered my life, let's just say, that alleviated the need to wear nightgowns to bed.

Because I decided I wanted to experience more in my life, I also decided to change my perspective regarding myself, my husband and my marriage. That was the beginning of the change I talked about in the last chapter. I thank God for bringing Mrs. Washington into my life for that 30-minute encounter. I knew that experience was a divine appointment. Thank you, Mrs. Washington, wherever you are.

A few weeks after this conversation, my brother discovered that his marriage was ending. He was so devastated. I think I was more hurt by his impending divorce than he was. He had what I thought was a solid marriage, so his distress was extremely painful to me.

During this time, I made up my mind that I did not want to feel that pain nor did I want my kids to have to feel it either. Don and I both decided that we would never bring up divorce again. No matter what circumstances came our way, we made up in our minds that we were going to work through the tough stuff. That perspective change was amazing! I can honestly say that the subject of divorce has not come up since.

While all of this was going on, I was diagnosed with extreme fatigue due to diabetes. My doctor gave me two options: take medications to control the diabetes or lose at least 40 pounds to rid my body of the diabetes. Guess what I did? Yes, your girl decided to lose the weight! Since I was going to be celebrating my 40th birthday the following year, I created a mantra, "40 by 40". My goal was to lose 40 pounds by my birthday.

I decided to start in January since my birthday was not until November. Immediately, I began to diligently work hard to make sure I ate healthy meals and walked every day. Later in the year, I even started running and surprisingly, ran my first race ever. By the end of the year, I'd lost a total of 53 pounds!

When I went to the follow up diabetic appointment, my doctor had tears in her eyes. My A1C number dropped two points and she pronounced I was no longer diabetic. She said I was the first patient to listen to her and to heal themselves of diabetes without any medication.

Seeing her joy showed me that changing my life had a profound effect on those I came in contact with. This was an awesome revelation for me. It motivated me to branch out into other things in the coming years. I took swim lessons and my husband bought me a bike. Surprisingly, I ran two marathons and completed two triathlons. Those two words were not even a part of my vocabulary before losing weight.

As my body was going through the physical changes to become well after years of neglect, so were my heart and mind. All of it was work and I would not lie to you and say, "I woke up like this." No ma'am, it took dedication and commitment.

I slowly stopped comparing myself to moms who worked outside the home as I began to see the value of me working inside my home. I actually started to love being home with the kids. We went on weekly field trips to Washington, DC and Baltimore, which my kids loved. I am thankful that I was home when my dad needed a comfortable place to rest after his kidney surgery.

I'm also thankful I was home when my brother and his kids needed me at the beginning of his divorce.

It was during that time, that I felt a hint of value in God's eyes. All He required of me was that I dust myself off, get back on my feet and fight for my life. My husband and children needed a victorious me, not a defeated one. I began to believe that God had great things in store for me and my family.

Before we realized it, our lifestyle became so hectic with everyone becoming more involved with their extra-curricular activities that I felt the need to pray again. Oh yeah, I forgot to tell you: my prayer life stopped abruptly too. I was so consumed by my life issues that I basically forgot to pray. My family stopped going to church and it reflected in our home life.

When I felt myself being pulled into my old habits of fussing about everything and arguing with my husband, I had to fight hard to get my mind in the right place. That place was where God could have reign in our marriage and home.

Whenever I felt arguments starting to rise up, I began to walk away from Don instead of "going there" with him. I also discovered that if I hugged or kissed him when tensions were flaring, this deescalated them very quickly. I would say to him, "You look mighty crazy trying to argue with someone who is trying to kiss or hug you."

Guess what? Soon, he started doing the same thing to me when I would try to argue with him about something. Eventually, the arguments began to dwindle down and were no longer explosive nor volatile.

Since our relationship was beginning to improve, I suggested we attend marriage counseling once more. Praise God, this time, Don agreed to go with an open mind. First, we initially attended sessions together until he eventually decided he wanted personal sessions for himself. He said he actually felt better after meeting with his counselor and that he received tools that helped him communicate more effectively with me.

Finally, he was able to relate his anger issues to his mother's absence from his life. He came home from one counseling session and cried profusely while attempting to apologize to me between heavy sobs. We hugged, cried and prayed together right in the middle of our family room. That was the turning point in our marriage. That was when the healing began to take place.

I was so excited about my life at that point. The beautiful thing about the process was that in the midst of me changing, my relationship with my husband began to change. It took 12 years for the light bulb to finally turn on in my heart and brain. I was determined that we were not going to continue with the same behaviors over again, expecting different results.

As my perspective changed, my life changed. As I began to see my husband as someone who needed me, I did not feel bitterness towards him anymore. I saw him as someone who needed compassion and understanding, not judgment and criticism. That made it much easier to love him even when he occasionally still hurt me with his words or actions.

Even though 2011 and 2012 were great years and led up to my marriage beginning to turn around, we had one situation that almost turned our marriage upside down. In the next chapter, I will share how, with God, we were able to work through that challenge to continue the healing process in our marriage.

Reflection

• Being totally honest with yourself: How has your negative thinking caused conflict in past relationships/friendships/marriage?

_____

_____

_____

• What can you change that will help you view your fiancé/husband in a positive way?

_____

_____

_____

• Write a list of at least seven things you love about him. Share that list with him.

_____

_____

_____

• Vow to change one thing you do or say that triggers negative emotions from your fiancé/husband.

Prayer

Father, forgive me for the moments when I had a bad attitude and a negative perspective concerning my marriage. Help me to humble myself to ask _____ for forgiveness.

Today, I take responsibility for the things I have said or done to create and/or prolong arguments. Remove negative thoughts that have resulted from my childhood or unhealthy relationships.

I choose to forgive _____ for anything he has said or done that hurt me, even if he did/does not ask me for forgiveness.

Thank you for your grace and mercy. Thank you for doing a new thing in my marriage. Thank you for changing me right now. I am no longer a hurt or bitter woman. I am the Proverbs 31 woman and my husband will one day call me "blessed."

I thank you that at this moment, you have given me a heart that declares, I love _____ unconditionally.

In Jesus' name, Amen!

Thoughts/Prayer Requests

6 Priorities: Let's Do It Again

"Motto for the bride and groom: We are a work in progress with a lifetime contract." —Phyllis Koss

How can imperfect people expect other imperfect people to be perfect? This is utterly insane and ludicrous. We constantly see this on social media. Society often places celebrities on a gigantic pedestal. When they say or do something out of character with the image we have of them, we immediately crucify them for their mistakes. We put ourselves in a place to be the judge and jury over them. To make matters worse, we do not forgive them for the perceived offenses that don't even have any effect on us.

The irrational thing about all of that is that we do not even personally know these people. We behave like spectators in a Roman coliseum. When we see the person brought in before the lions, we are shouting for the lions to win, never once showing compassion or empathy for that person. We often do this in our marriages too.

We can become disenchanted by focusing on our spouse's hurtful words and/or actions. Some of us become so burned out from all the arguments and disappointments, that we remove grace and mercy from our relationship. We oftentimes become hard-hearted, bitter and unforgiving towards our spouses.

I stopped making my marriage a priority and began to view it from a "What's in it for me?" perspective. I began to see Don as the enemy and not my friend. This was so unhealthy and draining, to the point where I became a married "zombie." I was there but I wasn't.

One day, I realized that we had become married zombies. We were going through the motions and began to get on each other's nerves again. I would say something to get on his nerves and he would retaliate with something a little more irritating. We eventually created a nasty cycle of constantly putting each other down, which would then result in days of not speaking to each other.

Is this your story? Well, girlfriend, I am raising my hand to let you know I understand. In the past, there were many times, when I would say that I had forgiven Don for hurting my feelings or for disappointing me, but deep down inside, I did not like him. How could I love somebody who would purposefully be downright mean and spiteful towards me all for the sake of getting back at me?

I can honestly admit, that if there was any little hint that he did something wrong in my eyes, I would literally be on stand-by with a lecture or some rude and condescending remark. That, my friend, was not forgiveness.

During those years of estrangement, I stopped making my marriage a priority in order to focus on me, my kids and the activities they were participating in. I threw myself into completing my bachelor's degree while home-schooling my kids. I was also focused on losing weight and looking sexy for myself, not for Don. I adopted the "I'm going to do me" attitude.

As I became more engrossed in my kids' lives along with achieving my personal goals, I became more detached from my husband. It got to a point where neither of us made any effort to make the other one nor our marriage a priority. This disconnect literally caused the unraveling of our marriage, while we idly stood by and watched it happen.

Years later, Don confided in me that he was stopping off at a bar on his way home from work. He needed to have a drink or two to delay coming home and to numb him from the arguments we often had when he walked through the door. He already knew that I would bombard him the minute he walked through the door with bills, kids, and complaints. Even though I was guilty of all the things he said, it still hurt my heart to hear it.

I turned his confession around and accused him of not only making excuses for his bad choices but also for having the audacity to try to blame his poor choices on me. Little did I know that I was causing the man I professed to love, much pain and agony. I had no idea he dreaded coming home to me.

I had no idea I was unloving, unforgiving and unkind for so many years. God had to humble me in those areas of my life and I am thankful that God showed me that I was not this perfect chick I envisioned myself to be.

Social media can be a good thing and social media can be a bad thing; need I say more? That is determined by how people use it. I love how it helped connect me to cousins who live far away, and how it currently is being used to help my older relatives keep up with what the younger generation is doing.

Folks who cannot attend class or family reunions are able to see the pics with the click of their mouse. I have even witnessed people rally behind folks who suffered sickness or death in the family. I know it can be used in wonderful ways.

I also have seen it used for all the wrong reasons. I can honestly say that when I was focusing entirely too much on me and my kids and not making my husband and our marriage a priority, I used social media in a way that almost ruined my marriage.

Right after I had those great revelations about how to make my marriage a priority again and before I could begin to actually get my life together, an ex-boyfriend from high school reached out to me via instant messaging. Every time I think about it, I am dumbfounded by how quick the enemy (devil) comes in to defeat you before you can get started on the right track.

I initially thought this guy's intentions were purely for nostalgia's sake, like all the other people I reconnected with from high school. He asked about my husband and kids, which I thought it was extremely sweet. I was impressed that he was interested in my family since he was newly engaged and had a gorgeous fiancée.

He thought it was great that I was not only self-employed but he also loved that I was a cheer coach, Girl

Scout troop leader, etc. He made comments such as, "I hope your husband appreciates all you do," and so you know I was flattered. I told him that I did not feel that Don appreciated anything I did for him or the kids. Eventually, he moved on to, "If I were your husband, I would make all your dreams come true" or "I would make you so happy if you were my wife." Again, I was naïve to the motive behind the compliments and to be honest—I loved them.

The reality was that he was telling me all the stuff my husband had not said to me in years. This fed a deep need that I had. I now realize I was craving to feel like I mattered and had value. It did not matter if I got that from my husband or from my cheer parents, I just desired to feel like I was needed and wanted. Even though Don and I were working on our marriage, we had layers upon layers of hurt and other junk to uncover and clean up, so I was vulnerable in this area.

My need for validation should have been met by God first and then my husband, but it wasn't. I had totally shut God out of this area of my life because I was focused on what I didn't have: attention, affection and love in my marriage. Don and I had become estranged even though we slept in the same bed every night.

This man materialized into that guy my husband had been saying for years that I should find to make me happy. My mama always said, "You best be careful what you ask for, because you just might get it." I got what Don had spoken to me in heated conversations—a guy who made me happy. I loved the conversations and how he made me feel. I started looking forward to meeting him on the chat. They were the highlight of my days.

The compliments continued for months without my husband knowing about them. I considered them to be harmless since I was asking him about his wedding plans. He complimented all the things I was doing with my family and we reminisced often about when we were in high school. I had no idea that this behavior would almost destroy my marriage.

A couple months after we started our instant messaging relationship, he asked to see me. He said it would be an honor to see me before his wedding since I was his first love. I graciously told him that was not possible, but he kept asking. In addition to pressing me to see him, his comments escalated to him saying what he could do for me in bed.

Once again, I did not shut him down during these conversations. On the contrary, I would instead brush them off by typing something like, "Well, that would never happen because I am married and you will be married in a few weeks." I never told my husband what was going on. I was in too deep! I was afraid of what his response would be due to his earlier reaction to reading my diary at the beginning of our marriage. Even though I was drawn into this guy's enticing words and loved all the attention and praise he was giving me, I felt trapped.

I finally dug up enough courage to tell him that his comments were making me uncomfortable and that I did not like the way his sexual innuendos made me feel. He apologized and promised never to say things like that to me again, but it was too late.

My husband happened to need to use the computer that same day. I had no idea I left my social media account open. Don unknowingly clicked on the tab and saw our chat thread. He read the chat in its entirety, from beginning to end. He was devastated.

We argued terribly that day. I was on the brink of an emotional break down because my family was in town for Thanksgiving and were staying at our home. We were upstairs having a war of words while everyone was downstairs enjoying being together.

At the end of the argument, Don threatened to leave. I begged him to stay, so he decided he would only stay for the kids and for my parents. I thanked him for choosing to stay until everyone left to go back home. I told him that if he still wanted to leave at that time, I would release him.

Even though we did not speak to each other, I prayed with all my heart and soul that God would throw me a lifeline. I did not want my marriage to be ruined by my terrible lapse in judgment.

After everyone left, we briefly talked about the chat conversations. Don said he could no longer trust me but he agreed to stay in the house long enough to figure out where he would move, since he wanted a "separation." He finally saw this situation as his "golden ticket" to get out of our marriage. The light bulb finally came on for me that I did love my husband and that I did not want my marriage to end. I wanted my marriage and I wanted my husband.

Through that ugly situation, God opened our eyes to the huge disconnect in our marriage. This ordeal also made the Bible verse that states that pride comes before the fall, real for me. It did not feel good to have my shortcomings exposed. It was painful to know that I had deeply hurt my husband with my indiscretion.

The beautiful thing about that whole situation is that God used it to knock me off my high horse and to show me that my poop stunk too. Up to that point in my marriage, I rationalized that I was a great wife who was loyal, and who took care of our kids and our home. That made me feel like I was better than my husband.

I can now admit that I scrutinized even the smallest thing that my husband did and that I also judged him harshly. That was wrong. I was claiming to be a good wife but during those early years, I was anything but that. I would compare him to my dad and remind him of all his shortcomings.

I appointed myself his judge and would punish my husband like he was a child. I would routinely deprive him of sex and give him the silent treatment—all indications of my immaturity. Initially, I was ashamed of these things, but I am thankful God forgave me and kept us together through all of this.

I am still amazed that instead of my husband holding that incident against me, he chose to show me such grace and mercy. Those are traits the old me clearly did not have. I, on the other hand, would be the one standing there with lighter fluid in hand, ready to make anything he said or did blow up in flames. I also used to frequently remind him of how he hurt me in the past with his words.

If the situation had been reversed, I know I would have been judgmental and unforgiving. Don was not. He forgave me and moved on. This, honey, is the direct result of years of praying. God proved to me in a big way that He heard my prayers. Through Don's forgiveness, I felt God's unwavering love. I continually praise God for this blessing.

I did not mean to get caught up in an emotional affair with another man, but it happened. I am extremely thankful that it opened up meaningful dialogue between us. Some of those conversations were heated and painful but very necessary for real healing to begin. I was finally free to tell my husband what I needed from him and how I felt neglected by him all those years. We both were able to acknowledge that we equally contributed to that happening.

We discussed how we stopped focusing on our marriage, years earlier and how we were more focused on satisfying our individual wants and needs. Without ever going to each other, we filled these voids in ways that made sense to us; not once praying nor seeking God for the answers we needed. I was looking for validation from my husband and that guy made himself available for that.

That ordeal gave us an opportunity to engage in candid discussions about how we both were hurting each other while in the midst of needing each other. Finally, Don was able to hear the pain and loneliness in my heart. I had a safe space to tell him how I needed him to directly say to me how much he loved me. I no longer would allow him to say, "You know I love you so, why do I have to say it?" Don agreed to actually verbalize that he loved me.

We talked about what we both needed: he needed sex more than once a week as well as down time after work. I needed him to give me his undivided attention, and to listen to me while I vented my frustrations, instead of him cutting me off and offering suggestions to my problems. We both agreed that we were craving for quiet time with each other.

For years, I demanded that we take the kids out to eat with us. I learned that sometimes my husband only wanted to go to dinner with me. I also had to choose to no longer bombard my husband when he came through the door after work. I gave him time to chill in front of the television. Because I removed the added pressure of dumping on him when he walked in the door from work, Don eventually stopped going to the bar on his way home.

God also gave me an awesome tool to effectively communicate with my husband. I finally realized that in order for me to help Don understand what I was saying and why, I had to write letters to him. Letter writing gave me the much needed time to pray before I got my thoughts together. I was also able to think about what I wanted to say and how I wanted to say it without being accusatory in my words.

Giving him the letters gave him time to process what I was feeling without putting pressure on him to respond right away. The letters eliminated all the emotional responses and arguments of the past. I am so thankful that God gave me the insight to write letters to my husband since that was one of the catalysts for healthy dialogue in our marriage.

Due to us actively being engaged in improving our relationship, we began to make each other the priority. That shifted how we saw each other. We began to date each other again. We started having fun again.

Our sex life was no longer boring or routine and it no longer felt like another thing to begrudgingly check off of my "to-do list." We began to pursue each other again like we did when we were dating. I knew this was all a direct result of answered prayers along with God's grace on our marriage.

At night, we now purposefully kiss before going to sleep. When I wake up, I have a sweet, new text message waiting for me from my husband. In the afternoons, Don receives a loving text from me to let him know I am thinking about him.

For the last few years, we have intentionally made a point to communicate daily about whatever may be bothering us. We try to take time out in the evening to encourage and to lift each other up. If we have something serious to discuss, we have times when we ask each other to listen to whatever is shared and not respond right away to what they heard.

This has been super helpful. The receiver of the information has time to process what they heard and now has the option to respond a few hours later or not at all. We are learning to be partners in effective communications in our marriage, which in turn, reduces stressful conversations and arguments.

Let me be clear: it took time for us to get to this point. We both had to agree to make better choices in our marriage that benefited the both of us. We had to: 1) respectfully listen to and hear what the other person was saying, even if we did not agree with it, 2) validate what the other person said, again even, if we did not agree with or understand it, 3) pray together after the conversation was over, 4) intentionally look to see how we could improve or change something that we were saying or doing to bring more positivity into our marriage, and last but not least, 5) spend more time with each other.

Most evenings, Don and I attempt to walk together after work to reconnect and talk without interruptions from our kids, who are now teenagers. We've even learned, on one occasion, that it is mighty difficult to have an argument in the middle of the street while your friendly neighbors are walking dogs and kids are joyfully riding by on their bikes.

Trust me, we are not perfect by any stretch of the imagination. We still have moments when things get heated, however, we are purposefully making conscious choices to be more understanding and forgiving to each other. We realize we both are a work in progress and that our marriage takes effort to be successful.

Now, we understand that we both have to intentionally put in the effort to carry each other's burdens. We make sure we apologize when we are wrong regardless if it takes a few hours to do so. We even decided we will no longer go to bed angry nor will anymore beds be taken apart in the middle of the night.

We are truly looking forward to the day when we will drop our son off at his college dorm and speed off without looking back. We are excited about spending even more time with each other. We decided we will continue to date each other to keep our marriage pleasurable and mutually enjoyable. Making each other a priority, substantially improved our marriage and I know when you guys do this, the same is possible for you.

My rationale for sharing our story in this book was to give you realistic tools to use in your marriage. I don't want you or any other couple to endure the many years of pain and frustration we lived with. I can truly say that I love Donald Barnett with all my heart.

If I had anything to change about my life as his wife, it would be that I had matured earlier in our marriage to save us so much unnecessary drama. Looking back over the last 17 years, I understand God allowed us to go through these experiences to now bless you and other couples. Knowing this makes every tear I shed worth it. You are worth it.

As you think about my story, I pray you will always remember that being a wife is real rewarding. Being a wife is a real ministry. Being a wife is a real gift. Being a wife is the real deal!

Reflection

• Are there things or people that are consuming your time? How can you change this?

_____

_____

_____

• Do you and your husband have time to spend with each other either in the mornings or evenings? If not, what can you eliminate to steal away at least 15 minutes to reconnect?

_____

_____

_____

• List at least five things you guys can do outside the home to reconnect that are fun and inexpensive and shows your husband that you believe he and your marriage are a priority in your busy life?

_____

_____

_____

Prayer

Father, thank you that I will not have to endure all of the pain and frustration Tanya and Don went through. I thank you for the information and practical tools I can implement today to have a happier marriage.

Even if _____ and I are not currently on one accord and have endured pain and frustration in our marriage, I believe that we are on one accord in the spirit. I declare that we both will equally give 100% to our marriage.

I will only speak what your Word says about me and my marriage. I will no longer entertain negative words from my family or girlfriends regarding my husband and/or my marriage. I will no longer entertain negative words about me. I am a wife, therefore, I am a good thing.

Thank you for transforming me into the woman of God you called me to be. Thank you for the Holy Spirit, who is my comforter and guide in those moments when I don't feel the love of my husband. Thank you for blessing me with all the tools I need to be a better me and the wife my husband needs. I will constantly read your Word regarding to my marriage?

I thank you that my husband only has eyes for me and that I only have eyes for him. I thank you that all hurtful words or deeds are forgivable. I forgive my husband for anything he has said or has done to hurt me. I am choosing to love him and see him how you see him: a child of God.

I thank you that you love us enough to allow _____ and me a fresh start as I speak these words at this very moment. I thank you that, TODAY, we can press the reset button and all things are new. I thank you that even now, my marriage is undergoing a 180 degree turn back to you. I declare my husband loves me like you love your church.

I declare, in Jesus' name, that I have unconditional love for_____. Your Word says nothing is impossible with you, therefore, I know my marriage can and will improve. I thank you that we will intentionally pray daily for each other and our marriage.

Give us more love and patience for each other. Help us choose to take on a new attitude and a new perspective regarding our relationship. Help us to make our marriage a priority.

Give us fun and inexpensive ways to spend time together. Thank you for blessing us with the gift of each other. Thank you for the gift of sex. I declare that we have a healthy and energetic sex life that we both enjoy. I declare that our sex life will remain fun and pleasurable as long as we are married.

Thank you that you complete our threefold cord so we will not be easily broken. I praise you for being in the midst of this marriage.

Thank you for making us a united front where we will raise godly children. Our marriage is an example of your great love and unending grace to our family and friends. Use our marriage to change our family and community.

In Jesus' name, Amen!

Thoughts/Prayer Requests

7 What's Next? You Guessed It, Homework!

"You can't go back and make a new start, but you can start right now and make a brand new ending." —James R. Sherman

Yes! Go you. You completed this book. I am celebrating you by doing my happy dance! Today is the beginning of a new chapter in your life. Mark this day on a calendar or in this book as the day you made a decision to improve yourself.

Since I am all about accountability and transparency, which I'm sure you know by now, I would love to hear your testimonies of how this book helped you. Please be sure to share any epiphanies or aha-moments. I love feedback.

For my single ladies, please share how this book opened your eyes to things you did not know about yourself. Share with me, on social media or email, what you are doing to prepare yourself to be a "good thing" for "Mr. Right." For my married friends, please share how this book not only impacted you but what you will do to improve your relationship with your husband.

I would love for you to share your victories or what you have learned about yourself via email, Facebook, Twitter and Instagram. Join the conversation at "Being a Wife Just Got Real" on Facebook and share your story.

Tweet parts of the book that resonated with you at @TanyasXchange. Tag cute pics of you and your fiancé/hubby on Instagram @TanyasXchange.

If you're interested in having me speak at your church or event, or hosting a book signing for Being a Wife Just Got Real, contact me at tanyasxchange@gmail.com.

Visit TanyasXchange.com to follow my blog and make sure I can find you by using the hashtags #BeingaWife and #realwifemovement. I believe, that together, we can change the world one marriage at a time. This is just the beginning of great days for not only you, but for your family, job and community.

Be Real. Be You.

Guess What?

We heard you and listened to your requests!

I've got great news for you who are thinking, "I wish my

honey had a book like this to read."

After much convincing (you know how that is),

Donald Barnett is currently writing:

Being a Husband Just Got Real

Visit my website **TanyasXchange.com** and follow me

on social media for more information.

Disclaimer:

I was never in an abusive relationship with my husband. It was highly dysfunctional and through what I shared in the book, we were able to grow and mature in spite of our issues.

If you are in an abusive relationship, you need to seek help immediately. No one should remain in a relationship where their safety or that of their children is at risk.

In the US: call the National Domestic Violence Hotline at
1-800-799-7233 (SAFE).

Made in the USA
Charleston, SC
21 May 2016